THE LIBRARY OF
AMERICAN
LIVES AND TIMES™

WILD BILL
HICKOK

Sharpshooter and U.S. Marshal of the Wild West

Joseph G. Rosa

The Rosen Publishing Group's
PowerPlus Books™
New York

JB
HICKOCK
ROSA

To the late Edith Harmon, grandniece of Wild Bill, who did more than anyone to preserve the Hickok family's history

Published in 2004 by The Rosen Publishing Group, Inc.
29 East 21st Street, New York, NY 10010

First Edition

Editor's Note: All quotations have been reproduced as they appeared in the letters and diaries from which they were borrowed. No correction was made to the inconsistent spelling that was common in that time period. On the cover and on page 30, images have been reversed.

Library of Congress Cataloging-in-Publication Data

Rosa, Joseph G.
Wild Bill Hickok : sharpshooter and U.S. marshal of the wild West / Joseph G. Rosa.
  v. cm. — (The library of American lives and times)
Includes bibliographical references (p.) and index.
Contents: "Wild Bill" — A frontier childhood (1837–1856) — "Bleeding Kansas" (1856–1861) — Civil War scout and spy (1861–1865) — Plainsman and Indian fighter (1866–1869) — Deputy U.S. Marshal and acting sheriff (1867–1871) — Marshal of Abilene (1871) — Showman and actor (1872–1874) — Gambler, celebrity and gold seeker (1874–1876) — The legend — Timeline.
ISBN 0-8239-6632-1 (lib. bdg.)
1. Hickok, Wild Bill, 1837–1876—Juvenile literature. 2. Peace officers—West (U.S.)—Biography—Juvenile literature. 3. Frontier and pioneer life—West (U.S.)—Juvenile literature. 4. West (U.S.)—Biography—Juvenile literature. [1. Hickok, Wild Bill, 1837–1876. 2. Peace officers. 3. Frontier and pioneer life—West (U.S.) 4. West (U.S.)—History—1860–1890.] I. Title. II. Series.
F594.H62 R679 2004
978'.02'092—dc21
                                   2002015368

Manufactured in the United States of America

CONTENTS

1. Wild Bill

On November 11, 1869, the Delaware, Ohio, *Gazette* declared that famous lawman James Butler "Wild Bill" Hickok, "whose name is reverenced among all cut-throatdom of the western border . . . is certainly one of the most remarkable characters of the age. . . . There is undoubtedly some of the wild romance of the border mixed up in his history, and he knows how to make the most of it."

The adventures of Wild Bill Hickok were first introduced to a national audience by columnist George Ward Nichols. Nichols, who had served as an aide to General William Tecumseh Sherman during the Civil War, met Hickok in the late summer of 1865, in the town of Springfield, Missouri. Hickok's tales of gunfights, manhunts, and spy missions, which were made of equal parts fact and fiction, captured Nichols's imagination, and Nichols decided to share Hickok's story with the country.

Opposite: Historians believe that this photograph of James Butler Hickok was taken in the early 1870s and that his sorrowful expression reflected his belief that he would soon die. Several years later, he was fatally shot as he played a game of cards in the No. 10 Saloon.

In an article that appeared in *Harper's New Monthly Magazine* in February 1867, Nichols described Hickok as 6 feet (1.8 m) tall, broad shouldered, and deep chested, with strong features and a pleasant manner. Wild Bill wore his hair shoulder length, and he carried two holstered Colt Navy revolvers.

Unaware of Hickok's gift for telling tall tales, Nichols recounted the hair-raising escapes and deadly shoot-outs with gamblers, Indians, and Confederate rebels that Wild Bill and his army friends had told the unsuspecting writer. Nichols marveled at Hickok's reputation for expert gunfighting, and he wrote, "Wild Bill with his own hands has killed hundreds of men. Of that I have not a doubt. 'He shoots to kill,' as they say on the border." Nichols continued, "Whenever I had met an officer or soldier who had served in the Southwest, I heard of Wild Bill and his exploits, until these stories became so frequent and of such an extraordinary character" that they "took shape in my mind as did Jack the Giant Killer or Sinbad the Sailor in childhood's days. . . . I have told his story precisely as it was told to me, confirmed in all important points by many witnesses; and I have no doubt of its truth."

Nichols was the victim of Hickok's sense of humor, and this largely fictitious article received nationwide attention. The public regarded it with a mix of admiration, disbelief, and anger. Wild Bill himself and many of his friends were amazed that George Ward Nichols had

HARPER'S
NEW MONTHLY MAGAZINE.
No. CCI.—FEBRUARY, 1867.—Vol. XXXIV.

WILD BILL.

SEVERAL months after the ending of the civil war I visited the city of Springfield in Southwest Missouri. Springfield is not a burgh | of extensive dimensions, yet it is the largest in that part of the State, and all roads lead to it— which is one reason why it was the *point d'ap-*

Entered according to Act of Congress, in the year 1867, by Harper and Brothers, in the Clerk's Office of the District Court for the Southern District of New York.

Vol. XXXIV.—No. 201.—T

Famous sketch artist Alfred R. Waud made a series of engravings to accompany George Ward Nichols's article in *Harper's New Monthly Magazine*. The engraving shown here was based on a photograph. Others were based on the imaginative stories told by Hickok's friends and by Hickok himself.

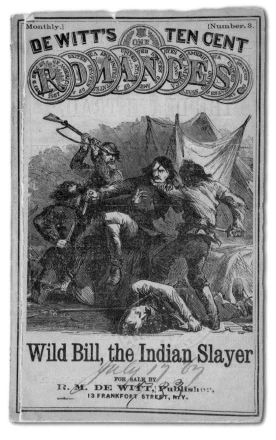

After the publication of Nichols's article, Wild Bill's fame spread. *Wild Bill, the Indian Slayer* was published as one of Robert De Witt's Ten Cent Romances in 1867. Throughout the late nineteenth century, dime novels were extremely popular. They offered short, simple adventure stories that pitted good against evil.

published such an outlandish account. The editor of the Springfield *Missouri Weekly Patriot* called Nichols a liar and accused him of printing only barroom gossip. The *Patriot* editor said that Nichols was guilty of "seriously endangering the supply of lager and corn whisky" by spending so much time listening to the kind of tall tales that were told in saloons. Yet the editor of the *Patriot* had nothing but praise for Wild Bill himself. He described Hickok as "a remarkable man," with great physical strength, personal courage, steady nerves, and superior skill with a pistol. He went on to say "no better horsemanship than his, could any man of the million Federal soldiers of the war, boast of; and few did better or more loyal service as soldiers during the war."

Hickok's fame spread, and he became known as a fearsome mankiller. He resented this reputation, but he knew that his own sense of humor was to blame. By the summer of 1867, a frustrated Hickok refused to talk to journalists, hoping to dampen the firestorm of publicity he had created with his own tall tales. The damage was already done, however. Stories spread of Hickok's bloody adventures. Today, tall stories such as the ones reported as fact by Nichols would be investigated. In Hickok's time, however, there was a great rivalry among reporters, and essential details would be left out or exaggerated to enhance an article. Nichols's stories, and the many like them that followed, helped to sell newspapers, magazines, and dime novels.

Today, more than 127 years after his death, Wild Bill's reputation as a deadly gunfighter and a crack shot survives. The stories that George Ward Nichols shared with the country in 1867 continue to give new life to the myth of the Wild West. Only recently have historians begun to uncover the truth by studying old court documents, firsthand accounts, and the work of some of the more reliable journalists. From these records, we can piece together the real story of James Butler "Wild Bill" Hickok. The truth, we have discovered, is just as complex and exciting as the legend.

2. A Frontier Childhood

Hailing from Stratford-upon-Avon, Warwickshire, England, William Hickocks, also known by the name Hitchcock, arrived in America in 1635. His descendants would spread across New England and be known by several spellings of the family name, including Hickok. The Hickok family supported the colonists during the American Revolution and fought against the British again in the War of 1812, yet they continued to take pride in their English roots. In 1801, William Alonzo Hickok was born in North Hero, Vermont. In 1829, William married a well-to-do young woman named Polly Butler, a native of Bennington, Vermont. The couple first settled in Vermont, then moved to Maine, New York, where their first child, Oliver, was born in 1830. Another boy, born in 1831, died in infancy. Their son Lorenzo was born in 1832. In 1833, the family moved to Bailey Point, Illinois, where a fourth son, Horace, was born in 1834. In 1836, the family made their final move, to Homer, Illinois, which in later years was renamed Troy Grove. Here, Polly gave birth to her fifth son, James Butler Hickok. The

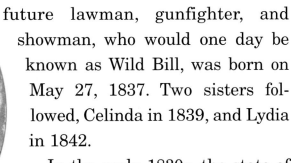

future lawman, gunfighter, and showman, who would one day be known as Wild Bill, was born on May 27, 1837. Two sisters followed, Celinda in 1839, and Lydia in 1842.

In the early 1830s, the state of Illinois was still part of the sparsely populated western frontier. White settlement of the area had been slow, discouraged by the fierce fighting of the Black Hawk War of 1832. Black Hawk was the chief of a faction of Sauk and Fox Indians. He

William Alonzo Hickok, father of Wild Bill, was very religious and dedicated to his family.

and his followers had refused to recognize the authority of two treaties, signed in 1804 and 1816, in which the Sauk and Fox nations had ceded some 50 million acres (20,234,282.1 ha) of tribal lands east of the Mississippi River to the U.S. government. This land included modern-day northwest Illinois, southern Wisconsin, and part of eastern Missouri. In 1832, Black Hawk's 1,000 followers, including men, women, children, and the elderly, had returned to their former homes along Illinois's Rock River to reclaim their land. The governor of Illinois had interpreted this

This image of Wild Bill's mother, Polly Butler Hickok, is believed to be from the mid-1860s.

Around 1836, William Alonzo Hickok built this house in Troy Grove, Illinois, for his growing family. James Butler Hickok was born in the house just months later.

gesture as an act of war, even though no warrior party would have chosen to travel with women and children. The U.S. government, under Superintendent of Indian Affairs William Clark, had then waged a fierce and brutal war on Black Hawk and his followers. The Indians had been starved, hunted down, and badly beaten. They had retreated north, to the valley of the Bad Axe River in Wisconsin, where they had been nearly destroyed by U.S. soldiers in a final massacre. Black Hawk had escaped, and his followers had surrendered, offering peace and

MA-KA-TAI-ME-SHE-KIA-KIAH
or
BLACK HAWK A SAUKIE BRAVE

PUBLISHED BY F. W. GREENOUGH PHILADA

Drawn Printed & coloured at I.T. Bowens Lithographic Establishment No. 94 Walnut St.

Entered according to act of Congress in the Year 1838 by F. Greenough in the Clerks office of the District court of the Eastern district of Penns.

forfeiting tribal lands in return for a guarantee of food and other provisions. The U.S. government had forced the Sauk and Fox nations to settle on a reservation alongside the Iowa River, paving the way for large-scale white settlement of the former Native American lands east of the Mississippi River. White settlers, among them William Alonzo Hickok and his wife, Polly Butler Hickok, had flooded into Illinois in great numbers.

In those early years, William kept a store, but when that failed he hired himself out to local farmers. The Hickok children helped with chores, but William and Polly ensured that James and his siblings also received a good education, both at home and in the village school. The family was close and hardworking. The Hickoks were staunch abolitionists. William and several local men ferried escaped slaves to safety by the chain of safehouses known as the Underground Railroad, often risking their own lives to secure freedom for others. Later, the Hickok family took in a young runaway named Hannah, who remained with the family for several years before marrying and moving away.

In January 1848, gold was discovered outside the small river town of Sacramento, California Territory. By 1849, thousands of gold seekers had descended upon the

Previous page: This lithograph of Indian leader Ma-ka-tai-me-she-kia-kiah, known among whites as Chief Black Hawk, was made in 1838, the year of his death. The fierce fighting of the Black Hawk War drove thousands of Indians to the West in search of refuge from the policies of the U.S. government, leaving the Midwest open for white settlement.

This fugitive slave, Hannah, lived with the Hickoks for some time. William Alonzo Hickok was an active abolitionist. He built a secret cellar to hide runaway slaves, who might stay for several days before continuing north.

California Territory, which had recently been ceded from Mexico. Sacramento was a rough-and-tumble town, and California was only an isolated wilderness, populated by missionaries, traders, and outlaws. The promise of wealth and danger tempted many young men to make the journey overland or by ship to the California Territory. In 1851, Oliver, the eldest Hickok son, left his home to join the thousands of gold seekers in California. Horace and Lorenzo were content to stay home in Illinois, but young James was eager to share in his brother's adventures.

In 1851, William Alonzo Hickok addressed his sons in a letter written during an out-of-town trip, saying, "James, I shall hope to have a good account of you when I get home. Horace, I depend much upon you in my absence [and] hope you and James will be friendly & steady & stay at home as much as possible & do all you

By the early 1850s, the question of slavery was an important political and social issue. Those who were opposed to slavery were called abolitionists. Often at great risk to themselves, the abolitionists did their utmost to help escaping slaves flee to states where they would be welcomed as free men and women. The routes slaves followed were kept secret and were given the name the Underground Railroad. Frequently, bounty hunters were paid a fee by states or plantation owners to recapture and return their slaves to them.

A barn on the Seth Marshall homestead in Painesville, Ohio, served as a hiding place for runaway slaves. This and hundreds of other stations on the Underground Railroad provided shelter, food, and rest to fugitive slaves on their journeys north to freedom. Most run-aways were healthy young men. Very few reached the end of the line, Canada. Many slaves were captured and were returned home. Others chose to settle in the upper Midwest or New England.

can for your Mother & be kind to the Girls." William's personal aside to James is the earliest recorded reference to James Hickok. In it, William acknowledges James's independent spirit. William's gentle request that James stay at home is in keeping with the Hickok family's recollections of James as a young man who preferred adventures in the outdoors to doing family chores. James often disappeared into the surrounding woods and practiced shooting targets with his first gun, which might have been a single-shot pistol, a shotgun, or a musket.

William Alonzo Hickok died on May 5, 1852, leaving his wife, Polly, to care for a large, young family. Although James helped with chores and worked for neighbors to earn money for the family, he yearned to follow in Oliver's footsteps and head west. Polly persuaded James to stay at home until he was a little older. By 1856, however, James was determined to leave home. The family agreed that James and his brother Lorenzo should travel west, to the newly created Kansas Territory, and try to lay claim to a piece of land on which the family could settle and farm. In June, the two brothers joined the thousands of eager settlers traveling west to the new territory.

3. Bleeding Kansas

In 1820, under the terms of the Missouri Compromise, the territory of Missouri was admitted as a state, and the new state government voted to allow slavery within its borders. The territory of Maine was admitted as a free state, meaning that slavery was prohibited there. A final condition of the compromise stated that slavery was illegal in new territories north of Missouri's southern border. In 1849, the California Territory applied for statehood with a constitution prohibiting slavery. If California's statehood were granted, proslavery congressmen argued, free-state politicians would outnumber proslavery representatives in Congress. Therefore, in September of the following year, a series of compromises was enacted. The Compromise of 1850 included a provision that the question of slavery in the territories of New Mexico and Utah would be solved by popular sovereignty, or the majority vote of the territorial residents.

In 1854, Senator Stephen A. Douglas proposed the organization of the territories of Kansas and Nebraska. On May 30, 1854, President Franklin Pierce signed the Kansas-Nebraska Act, opening the region to settlement

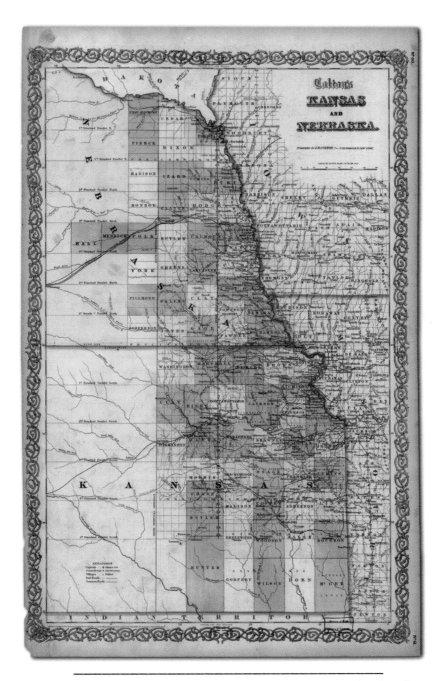

An 1855 map by J. H. Colton shows the new territories of Nebraska, to the north, and Kansas, to the south. The Kansas-Nebraska Act was perhaps the most significant law in pre–Civil War America. By opening Kansas and Nebraska to white settlement, the law intensified the division over slavery that erupted into the Civil War.

This Civil War-era etching was made by Confederate sympathizer Adalbert John Volck in 1863. In it, a group of jayhawkers led by Union soldier Charles Jennison attacks a proslavery community in Missouri. They burned homes, shot men, and kidnapped women. Similar illustrations from the time show Missouri border ruffians destroying abolitionist communities in Kansas.

and once again placing the issue of slavery in the hands of the voters. Within a year, the Kansas Territory, which was 200 miles (321.9 km) long by 700 miles (1,126.5 km) wide, had welcomed thousands of settlers, all eager to make lives for themselves on the frontier. The early years of the territorial government were filled with conflict, however. Kansas was a battleground between proslavery and antislavery people, known as border ruffians and jay-hawkers respectively, over its future as a slave or a free territory. It became known as Bleeding Kansas.

The question of slavery in Kansas was a crucial one. Slave-owning Missourians feared that, if Kansas became a free territory and later a free state, their slaves would flee to neighboring Kansas. Antislavery factions argued that too many compromises had already been made to maintain the fragile harmony between the North and the South. Slavery must be stopped, they argued. Proslavery forces from the state of Missouri crossed the border into Kansas and waged brutal attacks on the mostly antislavery Kansan citizens, earning themselves the nickname "border ruffians." In return, abolitionist organizations from the Northeast populated Kansas with like-minded settlers who would vote to outlaw slavery. Proslavery factions from Missouri nicknamed these Kansan abolitionists "jayhawkers," a popular term for thieves or slave stealers. Disputes between proslavery and antislavery groups grew and soon caused alarm among longtime Kansan residents and new settlers.

James and Lorenzo Hickok reached St. Louis, Missouri, in late June or early July 1856. A letter from home awaited them at the post office. The letter reported that their mother, Polly, was ill. James was convinced Polly's sudden illness was a ploy to convince her sons to return home, and he refused to give in. Lorenzo decided

---

Following spread: St. Louis, Missouri, sits on the west bank of the Mississippi River. Throughout the nineteenth century, St. Louis was a crossroads for explorers, fur traders, gold seekers, and frontier settlers. This lithograph was created by A. Janicke around 1859.

to return home, leaving James to go on alone by steamboat to Leavenworth, Kansas Territory, where he would begin his search for a good farm for the family amid the chaos of Bleeding Kansas.

In Leavenworth, James Hickok soon found employment as a plowman and day laborer. He was befriended by Isaac and Mary Cody, who lived on the outskirts of the town. Isaac had been stabbed by a proslavery ruffian some time before, and, following a kidney disease complicated by pneumonia, he died in April 1857. Mary Cody took in lodgers to help support her six children. Hickok befriended her eldest son, ten-year-old William. The two would become lifelong friends.

In 1827, Colonel Henry Leavenworth founded Fort Leavenworth on the Missouri River. The fort helped to maintain the peace between the local Native Americans and the arriving white settlers. In 1854, the town of Leavenworth, shown here, was built nearby. The first city in the state of Kansas, it soon became an important stop on the road west.

Few of James's letters to his family in Illinois have survived. In September 1856, he wrote to his mother that he had "seen since I have been here sites that would make the wickedest hearts sick[,] believe me mother[,] for what I say is true." On November 24, he wrote at length to his brother Horace, who had offered to visit Kansas to go hunting with his brother. James responded, "You don't get up early enough and you never scouted any so you could not hunt well at night." James, by contrast, was becoming a knowledgeable frontiersman.

In late December 1856 or early January 1857, James joined Englishman Robert H. Williams's western expedition to the future site of the village of Monticello, Kansas. The site stood about 25 miles (40.2 km) from Leavenworth. Monticello soon attracted white settlers, and James Hickok also made his home there. In Monticello, Hickok befriended John Owen, a white trader who had married into the Shawnee Indian nation. Owen and his Shawnee wife, Patinuxa, had a teenage daughter named Mary. During Hickok's stay in Monticello, Mary and James became very fond of each other. When Polly Hickok learned of the interracial relationship from James's letters, she sent Lorenzo to Kansas to discourage any thoughts of marriage. Reluctantly, James ended his friendship with Mary but remained in Monticello.

While a resident of Monticello, James Hickok came to be known as William, but no one has been able to uncover the reason why. The first written record of this occurred in the Kansas *Weekly Herald*. On January 30, 1858, the newspaper mentioned a forthcoming St. Valentine's Day dance, to be held in Monticello. A "William Hickok" was mentioned as a member of the event's Committee of Invitation.

In March 1858, an election was held for township positions, and James was elected one of four constables to serve under the local magistrates of Johnson County. Surviving court documents from this time identify him as James Hickok and as William Hickok. As a constable, James delivered court documents. On August 14, he wrote to his family that he had been to Lecompton, Kansas Territory, as a court witness.

In an undated letter written in Kansas, James described watching a public fistfight. In the frontier West of the 1850s, violent public disagreements were common but nevertheless attracted a crowd of interested onlookers. James wrote, "[Y]ou dont [know] what a Country this is for drinking and fighting but I hope it will be different some time and I [know] in reason that [it] will when the Law is put in force." James realized that it would be some time before it was safe for women and children to live in Kansas. The West needed lawmen.

During his tenure as constable, James acquired a claim to 160 acres (64.8 ha) of land, only to discover in the following months that a Wyandot Indian had registered a claim to the same parcel of land some time before.

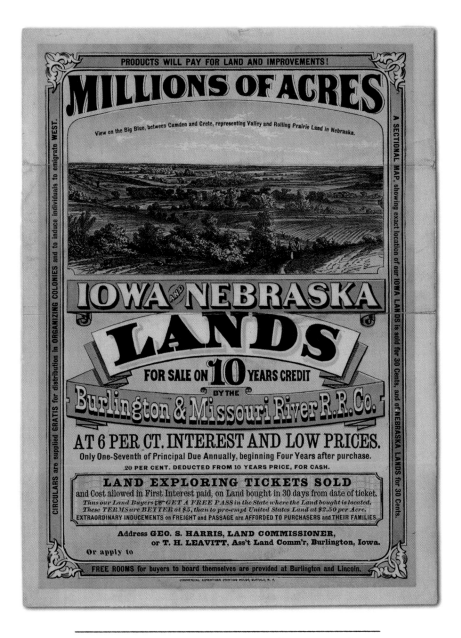

During the 1850s, towns sprang up across the western frontier, generally along railroad lines. When a company was contracted to build a railroad, the government paid it, in part, with large tracts of land, which could then be sold to settlers to raise money for construction. Eager to populate and protect their interests in the West, companies encouraged settlement through advertisements, such as the one shown here.

Prepared to start anew, Hickok moved to nearby Olathe, Kansas Territory, where his cousin Guy Butler was living. Bored and probably penniless, James joined the firm of Jones & Cartwright, a large freight company. Before the advent of widespread railroad networks in the far West, freight companies carried trade goods overland by horse-drawn and ox-drawn wagons. In his work as a teamster for Jones & Cartwright, Hickok traveled as far away as

The letterhead of the Jones & Cartwright company shows freight wagons traveling west to the Colorado Territory. The snow-capped mountain in the distance is Pike's Peak, then and now a landmark on the journey west.

Denver City, Colorado Territory, still an isolated rural outpost. The journey there and back would have been a rigorous one, beset on all sides with dangers and challenges. As a teamster, Hickok's job was to lead the team of mules, horses, or oxen that hauled the freight wagons. Early in 1859, James's brother Horace visited, but Horace, proving James's earlier criticism true, soon realized that he was not a frontiersman. After only a short stay, Horace left his brother and returned to Illinois.

Early in 1861, following only occasional letters from James, the family was alarmed to learn from cousin Guy Butler that James had died of pneumonia. Furthermore, Butler reported, Jones & Cartwright owed James money. Horace promptly wrote to the company only to learn that, as far as the employees of Jones & Cartwright knew, James was alive and well and had been paid off in late April. The company promised to send Horace's letter on to James's former wagon master, who might know where the young adventurer had gone. Though they were relieved to learn that James was still alive, the Hickok family nevertheless continued to worry about him. As it turned out, they had good reason to be concerned.

4. Civil War Scout and Spy

By the time James Hickok had been paid in full by Jones & Cartwright in late April 1861, social, economic, and geographic divisions over issues of slavery and states' rights had finally erupted into the American Civil War, the bloodiest conflict in the country's history. Most of the war was fought in the towns, cities, and fields of the eastern seaboard. On the East Coast, the Union and Confederate armies met on open stretches of farmland or wilderness and skirmished in the streets of southern hamlets. To the west, particularly in the hills of western Virginia, Tennessee, Kansas, Missouri, and part of Arkansas, a fierce guerrilla war was waged between proslavery and antislavery bands. While claiming allegiance to the Union or to the Confederacy, these brutal bands were often more concerned with plunder than with patriotism. Some men joined the guerrilla bands because they did not accept the discipline of an

---

Opposite: This tintype of Wild Bill was taken in 1863. In the nineteenth century, tintype photographs were easy to produce, inexpensive, and durable. Just before the exposure was taken, a mixture of chemicals was applied to a metal plate painted in black enamel. The metal plate gave the process its name.

army, and others joined because they enjoyed the brutality of guerrilla war.

James Hickok collected his wages and left his job at the firm of Jones & Cartwright. Before joining the civilian volunteers of the Union army, he traveled to Rock Creek, situated on the Little Blue River, 6 miles (9.7 km) from the town of Fairbury, Nebraska Territory. Hickok arrived at Rock Creek in late April or early May 1861.

Rock Creek had long served as a stopping place for travelers heading to the far West on overland routes, such as the Oregon Trail. At about the time of Hickok's arrival in the spring of 1861, the station owner, David McCanles, sold part of the Rock Creek station to the firm of Russell, Majors & Waddell. David McCanles was a rough man with a local reputation as a bully. Unbeknownst to Russell, Majors & Waddell, McCanles had fled his home state of North Carolina in 1859, with a bundle of stolen tax money. He had used the money to buy Rock Creek and later to send for his wife and children to join him. He had added some buildings to the property, which was then known as the East Rock Creek station, before selling the property to Russell, Majors & Waddell.

At that time, Russell, Majors & Waddell was the largest freight carrier in the West. The firm transported hardware, furniture, and other household necessities to settlers in the towns west of the Mississippi River. The company planned to establish Rock Creek as a relay station for their recently created Pony Express and had been

Historians believe this tintype was taken at Rock Creek station, in the Nebraska Territory, some time after Hickok's arrival in the spring of 1861. None of the figures in the image has been identified.

renting the property for some time. The company hired a man named Horace Wellman to manage the station. Hickok was hired by the firm or by Wellman himself to do odd jobs in the station's stables and stockyards.

By the time James Hickok arrived at Rock Creek, however, the firm of Russell, Majors & Waddell was in financial straits. The firm had purchased Rock Creek station by means of a down payment, with an agreement to make additional monthly payments on the property. However, the freight firm found that it could not manage to pay the monthly balance on the cost of the station.

In June 1861, McCanles persuaded Horace Wellman to go to Russell, Majors & Waddell's office in Brownville, Nebraska Territory, to find out why recent monthly payments had not been made. Wellman was accompanied by

McCanles's twelve-year-old son, William Monroe McCanles, who had errands to run at Brownville on his father's behalf. The pair returned on July 11, and Wellman reported that he had been unable to collect any part of the overdue payments from the delinquent firm. Russell, Majors & Waddell was bankrupt.

On the afternoon of July 12, David McCanles himself arrived at Rock Creek station, accompanied by two men and his twelve-year-old son William. Leaving his companions at the barn with the horses, McCanles and his son walked toward the house, where McCanles demanded that Wellman surrender the property to him. Wellman protested that he had no authority to give over the land, and an argument broke out between the two men. Wellman retreated inside while McCanles argued with the stationkeeper's common-law wife, Jane, in the doorway to the station house.

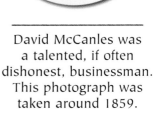

David McCanles was a talented, if often dishonest, businessman. This photograph was taken around 1859.

James Hickok appeared on the scene, and McCanles asked him for a drink of water. Hickok went into the house to get the drink. Moments later, a shot rang out, and McCanles fell dead. His son escaped into the brush and headed for home. McCanles's two companions ran from the barn toward the sound of gunfire, and initial reports told that both men were shot and wounded by either Wellman or Hickok. According to evidence that surfaced after the subsequent hearing, the stationkeeper's wife, Jane, then killed one of McCanles's men, James Woods, with a hoe, while the other, James Gordon, ran off into the brush, but was killed by the blast from a shotgun in the hands of someone else, possibly James W. "Doc" Brink, a Pony Express rider.

When William Monroe McCanles reached home, his family alerted the county sheriff, and Hickok, Wellman, and Brink were arrested and taken to Beatrice, Nebraska Territory, to stand trial. The three men were acquitted after a hearing held before T. M. Coulter, justice of the peace. Coulter determined that the murders of McCanles, Woods, and Gordon were done in defense of company property. The judge made no comment on the fact that, because of the outstanding payments on the property, McCanles still had some legal claim to the station.

The incident at Rock Creek might have been forgotten had it not been for George Ward Nichols's article in *Harper's New Monthly Magazine*, published in 1867. Nichols told a version of the McCanles Massacre, as it would be popularly called, in which James Hickok killed ten men single-handedly and suffered wounds himself. In the years that followed, Nichols's story of the fight at Rock Creek was repeated and would become one of the most popular tales of the Hickok legend.

On October 12, 1861, the *Illustrated London News* published this illustration of what they imagined a Pony Express rider to look like. The young man flees from Indian pursuers *(at right)* as he races over a Native American burial ground, suggested by the skull and funeral platform *(at left)*.

The Pony Express linked the eastern seaboard and the West Coast by an express mail service. With unheard-of speed, a series of riders could carry a letter from St. Joseph, Missouri, to Sacramento, California, in only ten days. Relay stations were set up along the 2,000-mile (3,218.7-km) route. The stations were placed 10 or 15 miles (16.1–24.1 km) apart, and, pausing for only minutes, riders would change horses or stop to rest while another rider continued. The horses were carefully selected, because the riders relied upon their mounts to be swift and surefooted both in daylight and at night. Only letters or lightweight packages were carried, and, for protection from hostile Indians, each rider was armed with one Colt revolver.

Historians disagree over who killed David McCanles, James Woods, and James Gordon. Evidence suggests that the bullet that killed McCanles was fired from inside the house, and that both Hickok and Wellman were inside when the shot rang out. Influenced by later accounts of the event, many people believe the shooter was the notorious Hickok. However, others argue that Wellman had a greater motive for murder. McCanles had recently accused Wellman's father-in-law of theft and had beaten him. Wellman might have been driven by vengeance to commit the murder. Today, even after considering all the evidence, historians are no nearer to the truth.

Some weeks after being found not guilty of murder, Hickok signed on as a civilian scout for the Union army at Fort Leavenworth, Kansas. Later that year, his brother Lorenzo joined him, and both were promoted to the position of wagon master. During the Civil War, the army hired civilian wagon masters to transport food, guns, ammunition, and any other essentials either to various depots or directly to the troops. Most civilian wagon masters were former teamsters, and they were all experienced frontiersmen. Each of the Hickok brothers was in charge of a number of wagons and a group of teamsters. The wagons were usually pulled by mules that were controlled by the teamsters, one of whom rode the lead mule or walked alongside it. Driving the wagons through a war zone was a hazardous task. The wagon teams were on guard against attack from enemy troops and guerrillas

A page from the court records of the Rock Creek hearing, dated July 13, 1861, identifies Hickok as "Dutch Bill," as indicated by blue brackets. In this document, Justice of the Peace T. M. Coulter records the testimony of Leroy McCanles, David McCanles's brother, who accuses Hickok and the other two defendants of murder.

anxious to steal scarce supplies. They also risked severe weather and other natural dangers.

The Hickok brothers were both employed in Missouri, but they rarely met during the war. James worked between the towns of Rolla and Springfield. Lorenzo wrote home regularly, and he reported on James's movements when he could. Only one letter written by James during this period has been found. Written in July 1862, to his sister Lydia, James confirmed his loyalty to the Union and described the difficulties he encountered when supplies destined for General Samuel R. Curtis, Union commander in the Southwest, were captured by Confederate troops, but he added no further details.

Many of James Hickok's Civil War adventures, as related by George Ward Nichols in his *Harper's* article, are alleged to have taken place between September 1862 and the fall of 1863. Some historians have concluded that the narrow escapes and dangerous missions described in *Harper's* were simply stories made up by Hickok himself, and perhaps some stories were just tall tales. However, it is true that, between late 1863 and early 1864, James Hickok was employed as a "special policeman" by the provost marshal, the military head of police. One of Hickok's duties as a special policeman was to report on Confederate troop movements from behind enemy lines. By early 1864, Hickok had asked to be transferred to the position of a scout, and Brigadier General John B. Sanborn eagerly hired him. Sanborn was in command of the District of Southwest Missouri, based in Springfield. Hickok was supplied with a horse, a saddle, and a pair of pistols, among other basic provisions. He was also paid the substantial sum of $5 per day, while soldiers earned about $13 per month. Scouts served in the vanguard of an advancing army, exploring ahead of the moving troops to determine the safest route of passage or the best method of attack or retreat. Hickok's experiences as a guide, hunter, and frontiersman would have made him well prepared for the job of a scout. Hickok proved invaluable to Sanborn, who later described Hickok as the best man he had. The Civil War ended on April 9, 1865, but James Hickok and some other scouts were kept on duty for two more months. They were sent to search out and report on Confederate troops that might either be unaware of the war's end or refuse to surrender. On June 9, Hickok was dropped from the roll of scouts and paid in full.

By the war's end, James Hickok, or William Hickok as he was sometimes named in military documents, had earned the famous nickname Wild Bill. It is believed that the name was fastened on him by fellow scouts and Union soldiers in recognition of his bravery in the field.

The end of the Civil War ushered in a period of national uncertainty. The return of discharged soldiers and civilian employees to their homes led to large-scale unemployment and unrest. The nation had to adjust to a peacetime existence and to the presence of a newly emancipated black population. As did so many others,

Hickok needed to find a job. Unemployed and facing an uncertain future, he occupied much of his time by gambling, which became a kind of occupation in itself for Wild Bill.

Toward the close of the war, Hickok had become friends with an ex-Confederate soldier named David K. Tutt. On July 20, 1865, in a gambling house in Springfield, Missouri, Hickok and Tutt met for a game of cards. At some point in the night, the two men disagreed over a debt Hickok owed Tutt from a previous card game.

David K. Tutt rises from the card table and threatens Wild Bill Hickok in this W. Jewett engraving from *Harper's New Monthly Magazine*. The image was one of several created for and included in George Ward Nichols's 1867 article about Wild Bill.

Tutt claimed that Hickok owed him $35, while Hickok claimed that the debt was for only $25. Tutt picked up Hickok's prized Waltham pocket watch from the table and announced that he would not return it until Wild Bill paid his debt. Despite their friendship and the intervention of their mutual friends, neither man would back down. Late on the afternoon of July 21, Tutt walked onto the Springfield public square wearing Hickok's watch. The act was a further challenge to Hickok's honor. Wild Bill called to Tutt, telling him to stop walking. In response, Tutt swiftly drew his pistol, and Wild Bill did the same. The two men fired at the same moment. Tutt missed, but Hickok's crack shot struck Tutt in the heart and killed him.

Arrested and charged with manslaughter, a regretful Wild Bill was put on trial. Of the shoot-out Hickok would later be reported as saying:

> *I had rather not have killed him, for I want ter settle down quiet here now. But thar's been hard feeling between us a long while. I wanted ter keep out of that fight; but he tried to degrade me, and I couldn't stand that, you know, for I am a fighting man, you know.*

At the trial, witnesses agreed that neither man had wanted the fight. However, witnesses also remembered that Tutt had made public threats to Wild Bill, provoking him to defend himself from injury. The judge advised the jury

"ARE YOU SATISFIED?"

After fatally shooting David K. Tutt *(at right)*, Hickok turns his revolver on Tutt's friends, asking, "Are you satisfied?" according to the above caption. Tutt's friends raise their hands in surrender, not willing to challenge Hickok. This engraving was created for *Harper's New Monthly Magazine*.

that a man had the right to defend himself, and Hickok was acquitted. The shoot-out was not the first of its kind in the West, but, thanks to Nichols's 1867 *Harper's* article, it, too, became a part of the Hickok legend and one of the most famous western walk-and-draw duels.

5. Plainsman and Indian Fighter

In early 1866, the unemployed and unhappy people of the East were again traveling west in great numbers. As in the years before the war, overcrowding, unemployment, and poverty in the urban East and the promise of free land and untapped natural riches on the frontier spurred migration west. In the South, the war had nearly destroyed the region's fragile agricultural economy and had brought an end to the existing social and political framework of the slave society, forcing former slaves and former slave owners to start again. Native Americans looked on with anger as the railroads stretched west, and the overland trails grew crowded with settlers. White settlers built fences, towns, and cities on what the Indians had long regarded as their communal hunting grounds. In response, Native American bands attacked settlements, railroad camps, and traveling wagon trains. To protect its expanding empire, the U.S. government built forts, many close to well-known migration trails, but there were never enough troops to guard such a vast area.

John Gast's 1872 painting *American Progress* was a widely popular representation of white settlement in the West. The lithograph of the painting shown here was published by George A. Crofutt the following year. The floating female figure represents America. She wears the gold "star of empire" on her forehead, symbolizing America's ambitions to control all of the land between the Atlantic and Pacific Oceans. In her right hand, she carries a book, which represents research and study. From her left hand, she trails a telegraph wire, which would link the East Coast to the West Coast. In front of her, Native Americans flee from the approaching wagon trains and railroad cars of white settlers.

Fort Riley, Kansas, was an important stop on the road west. The military outpost welcomed many frontier settlers, but the majority of its permanent residents were rowdy soldiers, discontented with life on the frontier. John Gaddis made this watercolor painting of the fort and the surrounding countryside on May 5, 1862.

The U.S. government viewed the situation in the West with considerable concern.

In January 1866, Wild Bill was still in Springfield, Missouri, where he had appeared in court as a witness to a local shooting, when he received a request from his old quartermaster, Captain Richard Bentley Owen, to join him at Fort Riley, Kansas. Owen had been appointed assistant quartermaster at Fort Riley. Within days of his arrival at the fort, Hickok was hired as a government detective and promised a salary of $125 per month. As a government detective, Hickok was given the responsibility of recovering stolen horses and mules. He also would track down soldiers who had deserted, or abandoned, their posts at Fort Riley. Hickok's brother Lorenzo, who was employed at the fort as a wagon master, later recalled that James proved to be a skilled detective. In May, Wild Bill was detached from the fort, meaning he was sent away on a mission. He was ordered to guide General William Tecumseh Sherman, who was on a tour of inspection, to Fort Kearny in the Nebraska Territory. Hickok was then ordered to guide General John S. Pope and a party of civilians and troops to and from Santa Fe, New Mexico Territory. As had most plainsmen and teamsters, Hickok had a good knowledge of the country. He was familiar with the geography and the terrain of the vast area of land, the plants and animals of the West, and the dangers of the wilderness.

In September 1866, Hickok returned to Fort Riley. There he found the Seventh Cavalry, one of four new cavalry regiments created by Congress in July 1866, awaiting more recruits and officers. The Seventh Cavalry, along with the all-black Ninth and Tenth Regiments, under the command of General A. J. Smith, were to be stationed at various western posts to help restore order to the frontier. In December, Smith's new second in command, a Civil War veteran named Lieutenant Colonel George Armstrong Custer, arrived at Fort Riley. Custer retained his Civil War rank of

George Armstrong Custer graduated last in his 1861 class at West Point Military Academy but went on to fight in several major Civil War battles.

brevet major general, so he continued to be addressed as General.

By early 1867, the U.S. government, increasingly alarmed by reports of Indian attacks on white settlements in Kansas, ordered the military to take action. Major General Winfield Scott Hancock, with some 1,500 troops, among them Smith's Seventh Cavalry, left Fort Riley and marched into Kansas to protect remote settlements and to engage the hostile Indians. The army, unfamiliar with the country, hired civilian scouts, couriers, guides, and interpreters for the expedition, and Wild Bill was hired as a scout and courier.

As a scout, Wild Bill was responsible for finding grazing land for the army's horses and mules. He was also responsible for guiding the troops to their destinations by the safest and most direct routes. In his role as a courier, he was entrusted with reports, orders, and other documents to be carried swiftly between forts or to

Winfield Scott Hancock was a well-known Civil War veteran and a popular figure on the western frontier.

and from troops in the field. The journey between the army lines was beset by natural dangers and the threat of Indian attack. It was a job for a brave, quick, intelligent young man.

Wild Bill soon proved his worth. General Custer, who was in command of the mounted division during the expedition, described Hickok as "a Plainsman in every sense of the word, yet unlike any other of his class" and as a man whom few of his fellow scouts dared to cross because among them "his word was law." In February, George Ward Nichols's famous article on the adventures of Wild Bill appeared in *Harper's New Monthly Magazine*, unleashing a mild storm of publicity for the humble army scout. Wild Bill was featured in numerous fictional stories, including two stories in the new De Witt's Ten Cent Romances, which were inspired by the scout's appearance in *Harper's*.

Despite the efforts of troops and civilians alike, the army's campaign against the hostile Indian nations, known by its critics as Hancock's Indian War, proved a failure. The U.S. Army insisted theirs was a mission of peace, but the expedition's sheer size suggested it was a war party. The Indians, aware of their tactical disadvantage against the larger and better-equipped U.S. Army, avoided direct contact with the troops and refused to negotiate. Hickok left his post as scout and courier in the summer of 1867, after which Hancock's Indian War became a conflict of swift guerrilla war and general disorder that would continue for many months. In October 1867, a fragile peace was established following a meeting between Indian agents, the U.S. Army, and Native American chiefs at Medicine Lodge, Kansas. One year later, in August 1868, however, the Indians would resume their campaign against white settlements, and Wild Bill would again be hired as a scout, this time for the Tenth Cavalry.

Serving alongside Wild Bill under the command of the Tenth Cavalry was William F. Cody. Cody was no longer the ten-year-old boy Hickok had met about fifteen years before in Leavenworth, Kansas. He had grown up on the frontier, hunting Kansan buffalo for the track-laying crews of the Union Pacific Railway Company, Eastern Division, and working as a frontier guide. An experienced plainsman known widely as Buffalo Bill, Cody had joined the civilian ranks of the army and was serving as a scout. The two men revived their friendship and remained close for many years.

6. Deputy U.S. Marshal and Acting Sheriff

Throughout his service as a scout and courier for the U.S. Army, James "Wild Bill" Hickok was also working as a deputy U.S. marshal in the state of Kansas. In August 1867, the newly appointed marshal for the district of Kansas, Charles C. Whiting, chose Hickok for the post. The office of U.S. marshal had been created by an act of Congress in 1789. In Hickok's day, as is the case today, the president appointed U.S. marshals. A marshal was assigned to a district that covered all or part of a state or a territory. The marshal appointed deputies who, in the early days of the nation, were paid fees for serving warrants and subpoenas and were entitled to receive rewards for the capture of army deserters. Marshals were charged with retrieving stolen government property, such as horses and mules, carrying out statewide investigations, making arrests, and handling prisoners. They also were in charge of taking the national census and of distributing presidential proclamations. Today, many of the tasks once performed by the marshals are performed by the Federal Bureau of Investigation and other agencies. However, the

Deputy U.S. Marshal James Butler Hickok, indicated by a blue circle, posed for this photograph at Fort Harker in September 1867. Hickok was a regular visitor to the fort, where he enjoyed gathering with the soldiers and sharing gossip at the local store.

U.S. Marshals Service still remains very active in federal and judicial matters. In Hickok's day, the job was a part-time obligation, and it allowed Hickok to pursue other professions, including that of army scout and courier.

Many of the early records involving deputy U.S. marshals have been lost or destroyed, but some of those relating to Wild Bill have survived. Records show that between August 1867 and early 1870, he was involved in cases dealing with the sale of whiskey without a license, the counterfeiting of U.S. currency, the theft of timber from government lands, and the desertion of soldiers. One man in Junction City, Kansas, made the mistake of passing a counterfeit note to Hickok, who pursued him to Abilene, Kansas, and arrested him.

This warrant was issued in 1869 by the U.S. commissioner for the District of Kansas for the arrest of John Hobbs, who was accused of stealing timber from government land. Deputy U.S. Marshal James Butler Hickok arrested Hobbs, and the warrant bears Hickok's signature at the bottom.

In the summer of 1869, Hickok answered the call of the citizens of Hays City, Kansas, who were in desperate need of a county sheriff. Hays City, today known as Hays, is located in Ellis County, Kansas. The city had been founded in 1867, and had been built on land purchased from the Union Pacific Railway Company, Eastern Division. The dusty town soon had become the haunt of buffalo hunters, soldiers from nearby Fort Hays, gamblers, and various questionable characters, few of whom had much respect for the law. Several local men had been hired as police, and, late in 1867, the first election for sheriff of Ellis County had been held. When the newly elected sheriff had mysteriously disappeared, a second election was held, and within months this second new sheriff also left, only to be discovered some time later running a saloon in Newton, Kansas. In July 1869, the citizens of Hays City petitioned the governor to appoint a sheriff. The governor ignored their request, so in late August of that year the county commissioners and the local vigilance committee held a third election. Wild Bill Hickok was elected acting sheriff until the official county elections in November.

Within days of Hickok's election, the city faced a minor crisis. A man named Bill Mulvey, drunk and hot-tempered, opened fire on frightened citizens with the intent of killing them. Hickok rushed to the scene and ordered Mulvey to surrender his pistol. Mulvey refused.

Wild Bill posed for this photograph at E. E. Henry's studio in Leavenworth, Kansas, sometime in 1867 or 1868, during his service as a deputy U.S. marshal. Hickok would serve as a deputy marshal until 1870, but his duties in this position were varied and irregular, giving him time to pursue other employment and get into reckless adventures with friends.

Some reports suggest that Mulvey aimed his pistol at Hickok and that Wild Bill was forced to shoot him. Mulvey died from his wound soon afterward. In late September, Samuel O. Strawhun and others who had been ordered to leave town by the vigilance committee invaded a saloon and threatened to kill anyone who interfered with their evening of drinking and fun. Wild Bill was sent for, and it was later reported that Strawhun attacked Hickok on his arrival. Strawhun was shot dead.

The law of the West gave certain freedoms to peace officers, men who were expected to defend themselves

Hays City had a reputation as a rough town when Wild Bill Hickok arrived, and it remained a violent town long after Hickok's departure. This grim scene shows the bodies of Privates Peter Welsh and George H. Summer of the Sixth U.S. Cavalry after they were killed by fellow trooper David Roberts in Hays City on September 6, 1873.

and others in an almost lawless society. Nevertheless, Hickok's actions always were investigated. He was required to testify before a coroner's jury about any on-duty shootings. The jury would examine the evidence to ensure that he had acted legally, either in self defense or in an attempt to protect others. The story that Wild Bill killed a man before breakfast every day was simply the work of an active imagination. Mulvey and Strawhun were the first men Hickok had killed in four years. Of the more than one hundred "bad men" he is alleged to have killed in the name of justice, only six men are actually known to have been killed by Wild Bill either in his official capacity as a peace officer or in personal combat. Though he regularly denied the truth of such outlandish claims, his reputation as a gunfighter did give Wild Bill an advantage over local troublemakers, who thought twice before challenging Hickok and his authority.

Wild Bill's reputation also attracted the attention of eastern tourists and newspaper correspondents. In the late 1860s, railroad companies began operating excursion trains to the West. These touring cars often stopped at Hays City, and eastern vacationers poured into the saloons and shops, where locals told tall tales to the tourists and fed their imaginations about the West. One local man is said to have claimed that Wild Bill lived on a diet of whiskey and the occasional raw buffalo steak. Tourism was good for business, and local storekeepers made the most of Wild Bill's reputation.

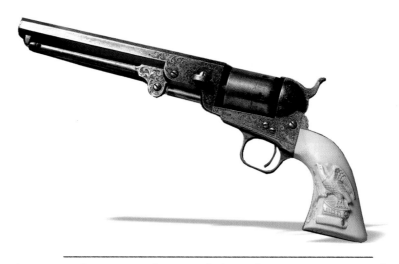

The 1851 Colt Navy revolver was light and easy to operate, making it a favorite of civilians. Wild Bill carried two revolvers at any given time. It is believed that this Colt revolver belonged to Wild Bill in 1869.

Eastern newspapers fed their readers' taste for western adventure, dotting their pages with detailed, romantic accounts of Wild Bill and other western heroes. On September 30, 1869, a correspondent for the Madison County Ohio *Union* reported meeting Wild Bill at an evening reception given for some tourists by General Custer and other officers at nearby Fort Hays. According to the newspaper's account, Hickok was dressed informally, and he carried his two Colt revolvers at his side and a large bowie knife thrust into his belt. The correspondent wrote, "Wild Bill is a regular frontier character, a desperado of no mild character, but entrusted with authority, [which] served no doubt a useful purpose in curbing the lawlessness of other desperadoes who regarded him as superior in shot and muscle to themselves." Elizabeth Custer, the general's wife and a great admirer of Hickok's, was later to recall that Wild Bill grew tired of such constant adulation and would disappear into a saloon once he knew tourists were about.

On November 2, 1869, Ellis County held elections for local and county positions. Wild Bill, a Republican in a predominantly Democratic region, lost to his deputy, Democrat Peter "Rattlesnake Pete" Lanihan, in the race for sheriff. Hickok's career as a sheriff was finished, but he would be long remembered by the people of Hays City and by the nation as an extraordinary peace officer. According to an article in the Leavenworth, Kansas *Daily Commercial* that appeared earlier that year, "Too much credit cannot be given to Wild Bill for his endeavour to rid this town of . . . dangerous characters." Hickok left Hays City in late December and moved to Topeka, Kansas, but, by July 1870, he returned to Hays City.

No one knows why Hickok returned to Hays City. He might have been on official business as a deputy U.S. marshal or just visiting friends. On the night of July 17, Hickok was enjoying the evening in a Hays City saloon when he was attacked by two Seventh Cavalry troopers, John

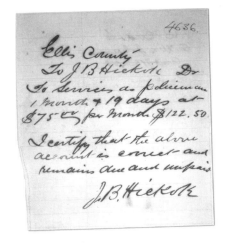

This is the only known record of Hickok's service as sheriff of Ellis County. The document states that the county owed Wild Bill $122.50 for his work. The signature at the bottom is not Hickok's. An unknown person signed Hickok's name.

Kile and Jeremiah Lonergan, who were both absent without leave from Fort Hays. Some witnesses later recalled that Kile and Lonergan were drunk, while others claimed that there had been bad feeling between the two troopers and Hickok.

Wild Bill was talking to the bartender when Lonergan came up behind Hickok, grabbed him around the neck, and pulled him to the floor, which prevented Hickok from reaching his pistols. As Wild Bill struggled to free himself, Kile drew his pistol, pushed the muzzle into Hickok's ear, and pulled the trigger. The gun misfired. Hickok, having by then drawn one of his own pistols, shot Lonergan through the knee. As Lonergan reeled in pain, Hickok broke free from the trooper's grasp, aimed his gun at Kile, and fired. Kile was fatally wounded and died in the Fort Hays hospital the next day. Lonergan was also hospitalized but eventually recovered and was returned to duty in late August. The Army took no action against Hickok, determining that the troopers were "shot in a drunken row and not in the line of duty."

Opinion was divided among citizens and soldiers over the cause of the shoot-out, but most people agreed that Hickok had acted in self-defense. Wild Bill continued his duties as a deputy U.S. marshal. In early 1871, he was living in Junction City, Kansas, when he learned that his name had been proposed for the job as marshal of Abilene, the infamous Kansan cow town.

7. Marshal of Abilene

The Texas longhorn of the mid-nineteenth century was a mammoth cow with a long history. The first longhorn was introduced to the Western Hemisphere by Christopher Columbus on his 1493 voyage to Haiti. In the early 1500s, Spanish colonists brought longhorns to what is now Mexico. During the following decades, Spanish priests ventured north to lands that are now California, Texas, and New Mexico to establish missions. They brought their hardy longhorns with them. These Texas longhorns, as they came to be called, were large, muscular, and capable of surviving the extreme weather on the plains of Texas. The herds prospered. By the early 1850s, Texan cattlemen had begun to drive their longhorns to stockyards in such faraway places as Louisiana, Missouri, Illinois, and Iowa, where they would be sold. The Civil War interrupted this profitable trade, but when Confederate veterans returned to their Texan ranches at the end of the war, they discovered that their cattle had survived and multiplied in their absence. By 1866, parts of Texas were overrun by longhorn cattle,

The Texas longhorn was well suited to the rugged conditions of the 1870s trail drives. Unlike other popular nineteenth-century cattle breeds, the longhorn had long legs and strong hooves. It was immune to many diseases, was easy to breed, and could thrive on even the dry pastures of the Great Plains. By the 1920s, the true longhorn was nearly extinct, having been bred with many other varieties of cattle.

and the cattlemen were anxious to establish an eastern market for their livestock. Transporting the cattle was the main obstacle, but it was soon solved by an enterprising young man from Illinois named Joseph Geiting McCoy. McCoy was a partner in a firm of cattle dealers. He realized that the cheapest and fastest route east would be by rail. He went to Kansas to find a shipping point on the railroad, and he discovered the town of Abilene. Abilene was a sleepy stagecoach stop that consisted of a few log huts and a saloon perched beside the

Union Pacific Railway Company, Eastern Division, railroad tracks. McCoy purchased land close to the tracks, and Union Pacific agreed to install a switch that would allow the cattle cars to be transferred to parallel rails alongside the cattle pens, from which cowboys could load the cattle onto the trains.

Joseph Geiting McCoy was raised on a farm in Illinois, surrounded by cattle and cattlemen.

McCoy envisioned the day when massive herds of longhorn cattle would be driven from the ranches of Texas to the railhead at Abilene along the famous Chisholm Trail. The trail, which was named for trader and frontiersman Jesse Chisholm, ran due north through Red River Station, through the Indian Territory, or present-day Oklahoma, and across the Washita, Canadian, North Canadian, and Cimarron Rivers before it ended in Wichita, Kansas. In 1867, the railroad did not pass through Wichita, so the cattlemen were forced to continue on to Abilene by the Abilene Trail, also called McCoy's Extension. The westward expansion of the rail lines would one day make the long-distance cattle drive a thing of the past, but, until

Following spread: Cowboys round up a large herd of cattle in this photochrom, which dates from about 1912. Historians are unsure how photochrom prints were made. The process was developed in 1890, and only one American firm was licensed to use it. When faster, less expensive methods of photography were developed, the details of the photochrom process were lost.

the mid-1870s, they were the big business of the West. Trails and extensions branched off from the Chisholm Trail and led ranchers and cowboys to such places as Wichita and Newton, Kansas, expanding the cattle business across the Great Plains. The Texas Cattle Trail went to Ellsworth, Kansas. The Western Trail connected Texas and Dodge City, Kansas. The Goodnight-Loving Trail went to Sedalia, Missouri.

The first shipment of Texan cattle left the rail yard in Abilene bound for the Chicago, Illinois, stockyards

on September 5, 1867. The cattle trade rejuvenated Texas economically and socially. Although some Kansans feared the cattle trade and the dangers of gambling and drinking which came with the presence of cowboys, others were prepared to ignore its failings and welcome the longhorns and the cowboys as they made the journey across the plains.

The cowboys who drove the cattle north to Abilene, and later to other Kansan cow towns, contributed a great deal to the settlement and future of the West.

Although regarded as laborers, they were skilled horsemen, expert with a lariat and good with a rifle but poor pistol shots. The cowboy's skills were borrowed from the Mexican vaqueros, or cowherds, who were themselves indebted to the ranchers of South America and Spain for their skills and techniques. The American cowboy learned to adapt his saddle and his tools to suit the demands of the American plains, and, by the 1860s, he considered himself the equal of any cowherd in the world. The life of a cowboy was not for the fainthearted. The longhorns were powerful, unpredictable animals, and stampedes were common and life threatening to

In the spring of 1867, when Joseph McCoy arrived in Abilene, Kansas, the town was a dusty community of one dozen log huts. McCoy built a shipping yard, a barn, and a small office. He then sent an employee south to spread the word among trail bosses and cowboys that the Abilene stockyards were open for business. The town grew quickly. An 1879 photograph of Abilene shows the sprawling town.

A group of cowboys and a local girl posed for this photograph in front of a bunkhouse in Willow Creek, Wyoming, around 1880. The cowboys wear the traditional costume of the cowherd, which usually included leather chaps and gloves, suspenders, a bandana, a wide-brimmed hat, and often a holstered pistol and an ammunition belt.

both cattle and cowboys. Life in camp along the trail was simple and rough. Social status in these new western communities was based largely on merit and skill, not aristocratic birth or skin color, as was the case in the more established communities of the East Coast. Though most cowboys were white, there were also large numbers of black cowboys and Mexican vaqueros working the Texas trails. In many ways, the West and the cowboys that inhabited it embodied the American ideals of courage and determination.

After enduring several exhausting months on the trail, with clouds of dust, pouring rains, and bad cooking, the cowboys would reach a cow town, such as Abilene. Cattle owners or foremen might stay at the Drover's Cottage, a large three-story building that served both as a hotel and a meeting place, but most of the cowboys slept in tents in camps set up outside of town, close to the cattle pens. During the summer of 1871, it was reported that five thousand cowboys were encamped outside Abilene.

The cowboys would want a bath, new clothes, and the chance to relax. With their wages, usually about $30 per month, in hand, they would visit the hotels, saloons, and gambling halls of the town. Many of them soon would be broke, having been virtually robbed by gamblers, cardsharps, and others who preyed on them. Tempers would flare, and pistol fights and fistfights were common, earning the cattlehands the nickname "murderous Texans."

According to the Topeka *Daily Commonwealth* of August 15, 1871, a Texan cowboy would use his revolvers "with as little hesitation on a man as on a wild animal. Such a character is dangerous and desperate, and each one generally has killed his man." There were, the writer added, "good and even honorable men among them, but run-away boys and men who find it too hot for them even in Texas join the cattle drovers and constitute a large proportion of them." In the summer of 1871, to protect ordinary citizens from these unsavory people and their activities, the Abilene city council moved most of the gambling dens and dance halls to an area south of the railroad tracks on the outskirts of the city. This rowdy neighborhood was known locally as McCoy's Addition.

In its early days as a cow town, Abilene had relied upon locally appointed policemen to keep order. In 1869, however, a number of prominent citizens presented a petition before a probate judge, requesting that the city be incorporated, or formally established. This request was granted, and the city was ranked a third-class city, which meant Abilene could hold elections for public offices, including the positions of marshal and county sheriff. The position of city marshal was created early in 1870, and the first man to hold the position was Thomas J. Smith. Smith was a good marshal, but he was murdered in the fall by two settlers who were later found guilty and sentenced to time in the state penitentiary. With the 1871 cattle season approaching, Abilene was in urgent need of a new marshal. Joseph McCoy, the father of the Abilene cattle trade, recently had been elected mayor. McCoy recommended Hickok for the position of marshal, and the council voted unanimously to hire Wild Bill. On April 15, 1871, James Butler Hickok became marshal of Abilene. As marshal, Hickok was paid a salary of $150 per month.

As marshal, Hickok was responsible for keeping law and order in the bustling cow town. He was also expected to see that the city was kept clean, meaning that the streets were swept, the chimneys were cleared, and the other tasks to protect the public's safety and hygiene were carried out. These public chores were generally given to the marshal's deputies, men chosen by the marshal and paid by the city council. Wild Bill's reputation as a deadly gunfighter and pistol shot helped him to keep order during the eight months he was Abilene's marshal. Few Texans wished to confront him, and outsiders noted that his presence helped to keep the place relatively quiet. At least once each day, he could be found at the railroad depot checking on new arrivals, and he patrolled the town streets during morning and evening. He was regularly seen walking down the center of the dusty streets so as to avoid possible ambush from a dark alley or window. Hickok also posted notices prohibiting the carrying of firearms in town. The state of Kansas itself had a law that forbade former Confederates from carrying arms in Kansas, but few former Confederates obeyed it. If either Hickok or his deputies found drunken Texans with firearms, the Texans were disarmed and sometimes locked in the local jail for the night.

Wild Bill carried two Colt Navy revolvers, openly displayed in holsters, as he had done in Hays City. He carried two primarily because the guns were percussion, or cap-and-ball, weapons. In later cartridge pistols, a self-contained bullet was simply pushed into each chamber, and then the gun could be fired. In a percussion pistol, every chamber had to be filled

Samuel Colt invented his revolving pistol in the 1830s. By the late 1850s, Colt had a factory in Hartford, Connecticut, and a second factory in London, England. The Navy revolver was an accurate, six-shot weapon that was popular both with the Army and the Navy. The gun became a favorite weapon on the frontier, where its balance and accuracy were valued by outlaws and lawmen alike. Some historians believe that it was called the Navy model because of its use by the U.S. Navy. Others think that the name was inspired by the engraving around the cylinder of the pistol, which illustrated an 1843 naval battle between Texan and Mexican ships.

with a measure of black gunpowder and a lead ball. The ball was rammed into the chamber with a lever attached to the barrel of the pistol. A small copper cap or cup, filled with an explosive, was placed on a small cone at the rear of the chamber. When struck by the pistol's hammer, the cap exploded, and a spark from the explosion set off the gunpowder in the chamber and discharged the bullet. Misfires were common because the explosives were often damp or otherwise faulty. Though he was a famously quick draw and an excellent shot, Wild Bill could not afford to take chances, so he carried two pistols.

Many people considered him to be one of the deadliest pistol shots in the West. Buffalo Bill said he had seen other men fire with greater accuracy, but none of them possessed Hickok's nerve and ability to get a pistol out and into action at such high speed. Those who actually saw him shoot at targets were impressed. It was generally agreed that Wild Bill could hit any target.

The cattle trade was a profitable business, but public opinion was set against the flood of rowdy cowboys, prompting the Abilene city council to take action. Late in the summer of 1871, the council ordered Hickok and his deputies to close the gambling houses, dance halls, and saloons in McCoy's Addition. The cattle season was almost over, but many Texans dawdled in town, spending time at the few saloons still open on Texas Street.

On October 5, at about 9:00 P.M., Phillip Coe, a Texan gambler, fired a shot outside the Alamo saloon on Abilene's Front Street. Wild Bill arrived to find Coe and about fifty armed and drunken Texans standing in the glare of the street's kerosene lamps. Hickok asked who had fired the shot. Coe said he had fired at a stray dog, and, as Wild Bill told him to put up, or surrender, his pistols, Coe fired twice at the marshal. Coe's first shot cut through Hickok's coat, and his second shot hit the wooden sidewalk between Hickok's legs.

Wild Bill, "as quick as thought," according to the editor of the Abilene *Chronicle*, drew his own pistols and shot Coe twice in the stomach. The Texans crowded around, and several more shots were fired. Another man armed with a revolver rushed into the circle of light toward Hickok. In the chaos of the fray, Hickok shot the armed man, too. When Wild Bill Hickok managed to gain control of the crowd and, with the help of his deputies and some citizens, to drive the Texans back to their cattle camps, he was horrified to discover that the second man he had shot was his friend Mike Williams. Williams, who had been a bartender in Kansas City, Missouri, had come to Abilene in the summer, leaving his wife back in Kansas City. He had worked for Hickok as a guard at the city jail for some time and had recently made plans to return to his wife and family in Kansas City when he joined Hickok's fight with Coe. Hickok gently carried Williams into the Alamo saloon and laid him on a billiard table, but

Williams was dead. Wild Bill was distraught over Williams's death. At his own expense, Hickok arranged for Williams's body to be shipped home to Kansas City for burial. Some months later, Wild Bill visited Williams's widow and explained what had happened in front of the Alamo saloon.

After Phillip Coe was shot, he was taken to his rooms and examined by doctors. They were unable to do anything for him, and he died three days later. His body was shipped back to Texas for burial. Residents of Abilene remembered Coe as a "very dangerous beast," and, on January 11, 1872, the editor of the Abilene *Chronicle*

The backroom of this western saloon was used for gaming. Some men gather around a roulette table, and others sit nearby playing cards. The gaming room of the Alamo saloon would have looked much like this.

SHOOTING AFFRAY.

Two Men Killed.

On last Thursday evening a number of men got on a "spree," and compelled several citizens and others to "stand treat," catching them on the street and carrying them upon their shoulders into the saloons. The crowd served the Marshal, commonly called "Wild Bill," in this manner. He treated, but told them that they must keep within the bounds of order or he would stop them. They kept on, until finally one of the crowd, named Phil. Coe, fired a revolver. The Marshal heard the report and knew at once that the leading spirits in the crowd, numbering probably fifty men, intended to get up a "fight." He immediately started to quell the affair and when he reached the Alamo saloon, in front of which the crowd had gathered, he was confronted by Coe, who said that he had fired the shot at a dog. Coe had his revolver in his hand, as had also other parties in the crowd. As quick as thought the Marshal drew two revolvers and both men fired almost simultaneously. Several shots were fired, during which Mike Williams, a policemen, came around the corner for the purpose of assisting the Marshal, and rushing between him and Coe received two of the shots intended for Coe. The whole affair was the work of an instant. The Marshal, surrounded by the crowd, and standing in the light, did not recognize Williams whose death he deeply regrets. Coe was shot through the stomach, the ball coming out through his

In an October 14, 1871, article in Abilene *Chronicle* entitled "Shooting Afray," Phillip Coe is described as "a gambler, but a man of natural good impulses in his better moments. It is said that he had a spite at Wild Bill and had threatened to kill him—which Bill believed he would do if he gave him the opportunity."

wrote that when Coe was shot nearly everybody said, "serves him right."

In late November 1871, Wild Bill traveled by train to Topeka, Kansas, for a short vacation, leaving his deputies in charge of Abilene. When he boarded the train, a companion warned him that five armed Texans, who had recently arrived at Abilene, had also been seen boarding the train. Over the course of the journey, Hickok moved to the rear of the last car of the train, to see if the Texans would follow, and then promptly fell asleep, leaving his companion to keep watch. Some time later, Hickok was awakened by a woman who warned him that a man, hiding a pistol under his coat, was sitting nearby. Hickok concluded that the Texans were following him and that they planned to avenge Coe's death. When the train reached Topeka, Hickok rose to leave, turned on the Texans, pulled his pistols, and forced them to remain on board the train as it steamed out of the depot, leaving Hickok behind. On November 30, the editor of the Abilene *Chronicle* declared that Hickok was "wholly justifiable in his conduct toward such a party."

In December 1871, the Abilene city council met to discuss the upcoming cattle season. The council decided to request those who "contemplated driving Texas cattle to Abilene the coming season, to seek some other point for shipment, as the inhabitants of Dickinson County will no longer submit to the evils of the trade." On December 13,

Wild Bill learned that the city council had decided to fire him and his deputies, because they felt that, having out-lawed the cattle trade, the town was no longer in need of the marshal's expensive services. The council then hired a new marshal for the reduced salary of $50 per month.

To many ordinary citizens, Hickok's presence in Abilene had been a great comfort. The editor of the Topeka *Daily Commonwealth*, in a tribute to Wild Bill that also appeared in the Abilene *Chronicle*, wrote that Hickok was "entitled to the thanks of law-abiding citi-zens throughout the State for the safety of life and property at Abilene, which has been secured, more through his daring, than any other agency." As late as the 1930s, elderly residents of Abilene attested to Hickok's skill as a peace officer.

8. Showman and Actor

Wild Bill Hickok left Abilene around the end of December 1871, and eventually traveled on to Kansas City, Missouri. Kansas City was one of the most prominent and prosperous towns in the Midwest and a stopping point on the trails and railroads heading west. Hickok, however, was drawn to the saloons and gambling halls that crowded Kansas City's dusty downtown streets.

Wild Bill boarded at the St. Nicholas Hotel, and, at about noon each day, he wandered down to the Marble Hall gambling establishment where he played faro, poker, and other card games. This routine continued until early July 1872, when Hickok was approached by Colonel Sidney Barnett, a Canadian who owned a kind of cultural history museum in Niagara Falls, Ontario. The museum claimed to showcase clothing, pottery, and weapons from all over the world. In an effort to attract American tourists to Canada, Barnett asked Hickok to act as the master of ceremonies for an exhibition called the Grand Buffalo Hunt, to be held at Niagara Falls.

In 1821, Francois Chouteau established a trading post 3 miles (4.8 km) below a wide bend in the Missouri River. Chouteau's community was the first non-Indian settlement in the area. The post quickly grew into the sprawling City of Kansas, later renamed Kansas City. By 1869, Kansas City appeared as it is shown in this drawing by A. Ruger.

Hickok accepted the offer. In addition, Barnett traveled extensively in the West to find Native Americans who were willing and able to participate in the performance. Barnett wanted to create a kind of circus that included Indians, Mexican vaqueros, buffalo, and Texas longhorn cattle. The vaqueros would give demonstrations of their riding skills and their ability to control the longhorn cattle. The Indians would chase the buffalo as if hunting them, and a military band would entertain the audience. This would not be the first such Wild West show, nor would it be the last. Barnett's great exhibition, presided over by Hickok, took place on August 28 and 30, 1872. Though the show was not a success, the public was thrilled to see Wild Bill, the celebrity of magazine articles and dime novels.

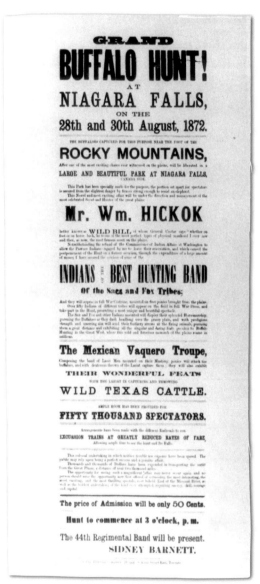

Back in Kansas City by early September, Hickok attended the annual state fair on September 27. The festivities were interrupted when drunk Texans ordered the bandmaster at gunpoint to play "Dixie," the anthem of the Confederate States of America. Some fairgoers protested, and the Texans pulled out their pistols. Fearing a brawl between northerners and southerners, Wild

A broadside for Sidney Barnett's Grand Buffalo Hunt advertised the displays of Indians, vaqueros, wild Texas cattle, and "Mr. Wm. Hickok." The price of admission was fifty cents, and the music of the 44th Regimental Band accompanied the performance.

Bill told the bandmaster to stop, and, though the Texans pointed "more than fifty pistols" at Hickok, he "came away unscathed," declared the Topeka, Kansas, *Daily Commonwealth* admiringly.

Shortly after this crowd-pleasing display of peace-keeping, it is believed that Hickok moved to Springfield, Missouri, where he was welcomed by old friends and fellow Civil War veterans. Wild Bill was still in Springfield in February 1873, when it was widely reported that he had been murdered by some Texans at Fort Dodge, Kansas. The news flashed across the West, and a number of touching obituaries had appeared before Hickok himself wrote to various newspapers from his hotel in Springfield, stating that he was very much alive and that "no Texan has, nor ever will 'corral William.'"

Still living in Springfield in late August 1873, Wild Bill received a letter from his old friend Buffalo Bill Cody. Cody offered Hickok a part in a theatrical production. Hickok would play himself onstage and would be paid handsomely for the work. Hickok accepted and joined Cody in New York.

Cody's theatrical career had begun in 1872, and had been inspired by the 1869 publication of *Buffalo Bill, King of the Border Men*, a novel about Cody written by Ned Buntline. Buntline was the author of several plays and dime novels that told stories of heroic western characters. He had met Cody in early 1869.

From left to right, Wild Bill Hickok, Texas Jack Omohundro, and Buffalo Bill Cody posed for this photograph while on tour with *The Scouts of the Plains*, from September 1873 to March 1874.

Buntline soon had persuaded Cody and Cody's friend John B. "Texas Jack" Omohundro to play themselves in Buntline's stage dramas. Cody and Omohundro had worked with Buntline until early 1873, when they created their own company and were joined by Wild Bill for the 1873–1874 season.

Dramatic plays based on the real and the imagined West had been staged for years. Cody's productions differed from early western theatricals in that living western heroes played themselves in Cody's shows. Under the general billing *The Scouts of the Plains*, a different play was chosen for each of Cody's performances. Each show was different, and so the production was called a combination. The company traveled throughout the eastern states and appeared in established theaters. Theater critics were not impressed, but the audiences, composed of both adults and children, were enthralled. Admission prices were low, the shows were raucous and fast paced, and every performance was sold out. Cody and Omohundro were delighted with their reception, but Wild Bill soon realized that he was not an actor. Despite his popularity with audiences, Hickok disliked the fictional presentation of the frontier West depicted in the stage plays. In March 1874, Hickok quit the show and returned to the real West. Wild Bill's departure saddened Cody and Omohundro, but they knew he would not change his mind. As parting gifts, they gave him some money and a pair of pistols.

A program for *The Scouts of the Plains* gives top billing to Buffalo Bill Cody. According to rumors, Wild Bill Hickok was jealous of Cody's stardom and, on one occasion, yelled at the spotlight operator for shining the light on Cody and not on Hickok. Other stories contributed to Hickok's reputation as a temperamental performer.

Back in Kansas City, Hickok discovered that the city council had ordered that most of the town's gambling establishments be closed in an effort to rid the town of outlaws, gamblers, and confidence men. For some weeks, Hickok earned money working as a guide for tourists and hunting parties across the plains. In the fall of 1874, he moved to Cheyenne, Wyoming Territory. Cheyenne, unlike the growing urban centers to the east, still allowed and even encouraged gambling within its city limits. Wild Bill made the city, and its many gambling halls, his home for the next year.

9. Gambler, Celebrity, and Gold Seeker

Cheyenne, Wyoming Territory, was a lively place. The city was crowded with dance halls and gambling houses, and it also attracted a large number of would-be gold seekers on the journey to the Black Hills of the Dakota Territory. Wild Bill is reported to have reached the city by train late one night and inexplicably disguised himself by wearing dark glasses, tucking his long hair up under his hat, and carrying a modified billiard cue as a cane.

In this unusual disguise, one story says, Wild Bill walked into a saloon and joined a game of poker. It was not long before he realized that he was being cheated. Hickok, acting more like an outlaw than a lawman, hit the dealer over the head with his billiard-cue cane, threw off his glasses, and pulled off his hat to let down his long hair. Wild Bill drew his pistols and advised everyone else to arm themselves. The cry went up, "It's Wild Bill!" and the crowd ran from the saloon. Hickok picked up the money from the table, accepted a drink from the bartender, and left. The following morning, the

The Metropolitan Billiard Hall, which historians believe was located in either Cheyenne, Wyoming Territory, or Denver, Colorado Territory, was one of the hundreds of gambling houses and dance halls scattered across the West. These establishments attracted sharpshooters, card-sharps, and thieves. This photograph was taken around 1874. It has been suggested that the fifth man from the left is Wild Bill Hickok.

owner of the saloon and the city marshal confronted Wild Bill. It was later reported that the three men came to an understanding over the distribution of the cash and retired to the saloon for a drink.

Once settled in Cheyenne, Wild Bill became a familiar fixture on the streets and in the barrooms, and his presence was noted in several out-of-state newspapers. Cheyenne's transient population of railroad workers and gold seekers also attracted much comment.

On November 18, 1874, the Omaha, Nebraska *Daily Bee* published a letter from a correspondent who suggested that the drunk and rowdy members of the population of Cheyenne be killed "for the good of the country." The correspondent noted that Wild Bill was in town, and he repeated the legend that Hickok had killed countless desperadoes when he was the marshal of Abilene. The *Daily Bee* columnist urged the Cheyenne authorities to hire Hickok, who, the writer claimed, would do more to bring peace to the town than "twenty such policemen as those now employed by the city." Hickok, however, had no intention of becoming a lawman again, preferring to play cards and hunt. His reputation as a gambler was mixed, but Hickok had acquired a passion for card playing in his youth, and he was enjoying the life of an idle card player. Though it was reported later in the year that Wild Bill would soon leave for the Black Hills of the Dakota Territory, he remained in Cheyenne until the summer of 1875.

In June 1875, Wild Bill was charged with vagrancy. He had no visible means of support and apparently no interest in or prospect of a steady job. Friends posted his bail, and the case never went to court. Cheyenne's residents defended Hickok, arguing that the charge was simply a ploy on the part of the city council to rid the town of supposedly dangerous people. However, Wild Bill let it be known that he would not be forced out of town by any civic authority.

On March 5, 1876, Wild Bill married Agnes Lake Thatcher, the widow of murdered circus owner William Lake Thatcher. Agnes was a circus performer as well, and she had met Wild Bill in 1871, when she had traveled to Abilene with her late husband's circus. Agnes and Wild Bill had corresponded regularly, and their marriage in Cheyenne was celebrated by Hickok's friends. After a short honeymoon, Wild Bill established Agnes in Cincinnati, Ohio, with the promise to send for her later. After traveling in the West for some months, Hickok returned to St. Louis, Missouri, where he announced his plans for an expedition to the Black Hills, raised a company, and gathered his supplies. From St. Louis he again headed west to Cheyenne, where he joined Charles "Colorado Charlie" Utter and a group of men bound for the Black Hills. The group set out for Deadwood, Dakota Territory, late in June, and they arrived in the frontier town several weeks later. On the way, they stopped at Fort Laramie, and it was there that Martha Jane Cannary, better known as Calamity Jane, joined the party. It is believed that Jane had been locked in the fort's guardhouse to recover from a bout

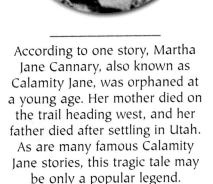

According to one story, Martha Jane Cannary, also known as Calamity Jane, was orphaned at a young age. Her mother died on the trail heading west, and her father died after settling in Utah. As are many famous Calamity Jane stories, this tragic tale may be only a popular legend.

As early as the 1830s, trappers reported finding gold in the Black Hills of the Dakota Territory, but little attention was paid to such reports. In 1868, the U.S. government set aside the territory as a reservation for the Sioux Indians. By the early 1870s, however, the U.S. Army was considering building a military post in the Black Hills, which would be used to protect white settlers if war with the Sioux broke out. General George Armstrong Custer was placed in charge of an expeditionary force to explore the area. Custer's force consisted of troops, wagons, an interpreter, and Indian guides. The Sioux were suspicious of the military but did not attack. On his return, Custer reported that large deposits of gold had been discovered in the region. Custer and the U.S. government wished to conceal the potentially profitable discovery, but the newspapermen who had accompanied the expedition soon publicized the information. Despite efforts by the military to repel white settlement and preserve the Indians' rights to the land, thousands of gold seekers invaded the Black Hills. By late 1875, illegal camps and townships had sprung up wherever gold had been found or was likely to be found. The large-scale white settlement of the Black Hills would lead to a war with the Sioux nation the following year.

of drunkenness, and Fort Laramie's post commander was anxious to be rid of her. The arrival of the Hickok-Utter party provided an ideal opportunity. Rumors would later have it that Calamity Jane and Wild Bill were married soon after this meeting and that the couple had a daughter together, but this claim has since been disproved.

Wild Bill Hickok and his party first caught sight of the rickety clapboard buildings of Deadwood, Dakota Territory, on July 11 or 12, 1876. Only a few months before, on April 28, 1876, a group of gold seekers had arrived at the base of an uninhabited canyon and tied up their horses for the night, naming their little camp Deadwood Gulch. The camp had grown into a dusty, tented city. Soon the tents had been replaced by wooden buildings set on either side of a winding street that weaved like a snake around tree stumps and wagon-wheel potholes. The town had come to be called simply Deadwood, and it would become the most famous mining camp in the West.

By the time Hickok and his friends arrived in July, Deadwood was a thriving place dominated by saloons and gambling houses together with some general stores and various other buildings. Wild Bill did little to attract attention to himself in Deadwood. In a letter to his wife dated July 17, Hickok assured Agnes that he spent most of his time prospecting for gold. However, residents of Deadwood later recalled that he spent

Deadwood, Dakota Territory, was named for the dead trees that dotted the canyon walls when the settlement's founders first arrived. By the summer of 1877, when this photograph was taken, the town's only street was crowded with gambling halls, general stores, and a bank.

more time at the gaming tables laying down bets than down at the creek panning for gold. On the evening of August 1, he played a game of poker with a group of friends and a young man named Jack McCall. McCall lost and was unable to pay his debt to Hickok, but promised to pay the next day. Before McCall left the saloon for the evening, Hickok lent him enough money to buy breakfast the following morning.

That evening, Wild Bill wrote a letter to his wife and included the haunting promise that, "if such should be that we never meet again, while firing my last shot, I will gently breathe the name of my wife–Agnes–and with wishes even for my enemies, I will make the plunge and try to swim to the other shore." Hickok seems to have had a sense of his impending death. Friends would later recall that, on more than one occasion, Hickok had expressed the belief that he would never leave the Black Hills alive.

Soon after noon the following day, August 2, Wild Bill entered the No. 10 Saloon and joined three friends in a game of poker. On this day, Charles Rich had taken Hickok's regular seat against the wall. The seat offered a view of both the front and back doors, giving its occupant a view of the entire saloon. Hickok reluctantly sat down in the only empty chair, with his back to the rear door and a view of the front door. At about 3:00 P.M., Jack McCall entered the saloon and wandered around the room. Suddenly, he approached Wild Bill from behind and shot him in the head with a Colt Navy revolver. Hickok died instantly. Several men lunged toward McCall, who aimed his pistol at them and pulled the trigger, but the gun refused to fire. McCall ran from the saloon but was caught some distance away and placed under guard.

When the shot that killed Wild Bill was fired, Captain William R. Massie, a former riverboat pilot, felt a numbness in his left wrist. Massie looked at Hickok, who was seated across the table, and assumed that Hickok had shot him. A moment later, however, Wild

Bill's lifeless body fell sideways to the floor, and Massie saw McCall, pistol in hand, threatening the crowd. Massie soon realized that the bullet that had killed Wild Bill had passed through Hickok's right cheekbone and embedded itself in Massie's wrist. For years afterward, Massie would offer people the opportunity to "shake the hand that once held the bullet that killed Wild Bill."

The next day, Jack McCall was placed on trial for murder. The case was tried before a hastily assembled jury composed of local gold miners whose names were picked out of a hat. Because Deadwood was built on what was still Native American land and therefore not under the authority of the U.S. government, the court had no legal authority. His captors, however, chose to try McCall in this mock court rather than release him to the public, many of whom were calling for his immediate execution. In the course of the trial, McCall claimed to have shot Wild Bill to avenge Hickok's murder of McCall's brother. This defense was a lie, but, despite the evidence, the jury returned a verdict of not guilty, and Jack McCall was released, much to the anger of many of the people present. Historians have since argued that the jury found McCall innocent to avoid the sticky legal question of hanging him without the authority of the U.S. government. According to the law of the Indian reservation on which Deadwood was built, McCall's captors should have handed him over to a deputy U.S. marshal. The deputy marshal would then have taken him to Yankton, Dakota Territory, where the court would have decided his fate under the authority of the federal court system.

Though a free man following the trial, McCall was by no means safe. When Moses Milner, better known as California Joe and one of Hickok's best friends, learned of Hickok's death, Milner tracked down McCall and threatened to kill him if McCall did not leave Deadwood immediately. A frantic McCall fled soon after, but he did not escape justice. On his return to the Wyoming Territory, he boasted of his deed, and he was arrested by a deputy U.S. marshal and was examined before a magistrate. The magistrate decided that McCall should stand trial for a crime committed on Indian land. Taken to Yankton, McCall was tried in early December 1876, was found guilty, and was hanged on March 1, 1877.

On August 3, 1876, Wild Bill was buried on the outskirts of Deadwood with his favorite rifle by his side. His funeral was attended by friends and a crowd of Deadwood residents. His wife, Agnes, would not visit the grave until the final months of 1877. News of Wild Bill's murder flashed across the West. Many Americans were initially skeptical, because Hickok had been reported dead several times before. This time, it was no tall tale, however. Hickok's death was described and mourned in local newspapers across the West. The editor

Charles "Colorado Charlie" Utter is seated beside Wild Bill's first grave, and Arapaho Joe poses beside it in this 1877 photograph.

By 1879, Deadwood had outgrown its first settlements, and it became necessary to move all the existing graves from the town's cemetery to a new one located on nearby Mount Moriah. Wild Bill's coffin was among the many removed and reburied. Before its reburial, the coffin was opened, and Hickok's friends looked once more on Wild Bill. They were amazed to see that he was still very lifelike. Chemicals in the soil had preserved his body. Charles "Colorado Charlie" Utter then removed Hickok's favorite rifle and closed the coffin for the last time.

of the Yankton, Dakota Territory, *Press & Dakotaian* memorialized Wild Bill and his remarkable career with the words:

> [A]s a fitting close to the tragic drama we may say of 'Wild Bill,' notwithstanding his eventful and exciting career as a scout of the Union army during the war, and on the frontier and the wild plains of the west, amongst wild and lawless whites, and still more savage redmen, he was still a quiet and unassuming man, peaceable and harmless, except when menaced by the cold glitter of the Bowie knife or the deadly muzzle of the revolver. At such times his nerve and cool daring were unparalleled. As a soldier, scout, marshal, sheriff and private citizen, his qualities enabled him always, by rapidity of execution and extraordinary fearlessness, to defeat and destroy his enemies when the odds were overwhelming . . . Though his life was bloody and adventurous, yet he was the champion of the weak and oppressed; and if he was not a paragon of excellence, he was at least a man of brave impulses.

10. The Legend

The day that the Hickok family heard the news of Wild Bill Hickok's death, they attempted to hide the news from his mother, Polly. Polly, however, realized that something was wrong, found a newspaper, and read of her son's death. Her daughter found her with the newspaper lying by her side as she rocked back and forth, tears streaming down her face. Some months after Wild Bill's death, his wife, Agnes, wrote to Polly, saying that the "longer he is Dead the worse I feel." Polly shared this sadness. She died in 1878, still mourning the death of her son.

Wild Bill Hickok left a remarkable imprint on American history. Much of what he actually achieved has been overshadowed by myth and legend. Of Wild Bill's adventures his sister Lydia later wrote, "When we were children he was always telling just such yarns to amuse the rest of us[.] we were always a great family to read aloud to each other." The stories of narrow escapes and countless murders, Lydia recalled, only made her laugh.

Yet Wild Bill's image as a law enforcer continues to attract attention amongst both historians and those for whom the Old West and its colorful characters will never die. Hickok's life has been honored and celebrated throughout the twentieth and twenty-first centuries. In 1943, one of the famous Liberty Ships of World War II, a series of cargo ships built to carry supplies to Allied troops in England, was christened the *James B. Hickok*. More recently, Hickok has been named a member of the patriotic organization the Sons of the American Revolution, an honor that would have made him very proud.

James Butler Hickok has now passed into legend, but his name will live on and his reputation will not fade. He was a man who shot straight, asked favors of no one, and courageously faced his enemies in defense of himself and others.

According to legend, the cards that Wild Bill was holding at the time of his death were aces and eights, a combination that became known as Deadman's Hand. Reports in the press following Hickok's death made no mention of the Deadman's Hand, but, in the 1920s, Ellis T. "Doc" Peirce, who had helped to prepare Wild Bill for burial, claimed that the cards were the ace of spades, the ace of clubs, the eight of clubs, the eight of spades, and either the queen or the jack of diamonds. There is no evidence to support this claim, but the hand has become a part of the Hickok legend.

Timeline

1837	May 27, James Butler Hickok is born at Homer, Illinois.
1852	William Alonzo Hickok, James's father, dies.
1856	James Hickok leaves home for the Kansas Territory.
1858	Hickok is elected a village constable in the town of Monticello, Kansas.
1859	Hickok becomes a teamster with the freight firm of Jones & Cartwright.
1861	On July 12, the McCanles fight occurs, and, in August, Hickok joins the Union army as a teamster. He later is promoted to wagon master.
1862–1865	Hickok serves as wagon master, scout, detective, and spy. He earns the nickname Wild Bill among his fellow scouts.
1865	On July 21, Hickok kills David K. Tutt in a duel. Hickok is tried for manslaughter and is acquitted.
1866	In January, Hickok is sent to Fort Riley, Kansas, where he is hired as a government detective. He also serves as a scout for Generals Sherman and Pope.
1867	Hickok is hired as a scout for the Seventh Cavalry during the 1867 Indian War and later is appointed a deputy U.S. marshal.
Aug. 1868–Feb. 1869	Hickok serves as a scout for the Tenth Cavalry.
1869	In August, Hickok is elected acting sheriff of Ellis County, Kansas. Later that month, he kills Bill Mulvey.
	On September 27, Hickok kills Samuel O. Strawhun during a saloon riot.

1870	On July 17, Hickok kills one soldier and wounds another when they attack him in a saloon at Hays City.
1871	On April 15, Hickok is appointed marshal of Abilene.
	On October 5, he is attacked by Texans. He kills one of them and friend Mike Williams by mistake.
	On December 13, Hickok and his deputies are dismissed, because Abilene is no longer in need of their services.
1872	In August, Hickok acts as a master of ceremonies at the Grand Buffalo Hunt at Niagara Falls, Ontario.
1873	In February, while in Springfield, Missouri, Hickok is incorrectly reported shot at Fort Dodge, Kansas.
	In August, Hickok is invited by Buffalo Bill to join his theatrical combination in New York.
1874	In March, Hickok leaves Cody, returns to Kansas City, and then moves on to Cheyenne, Wyoming Territory.
1875	In June, still at Cheyenne, Hickok is charged with vagrancy. He leaves Cheyenne and is believed to have gone to the Black Hills of Dakota Territory.
1876	On March 5, Hickok marries Agnes Lake Thatcher. He leaves her in Cincinnati, Ohio, and heads west to Deadwood with Charles "Colorado Charlie" Utter.
	On August 2, Hickok is shot by Jack McCall in Deadwood's No. 10 Saloon. The next day, Hickok is buried. McCall is tried by an illegal miners' court and is released.
	In September, McCall is arrested and is tried for murder. McCall is found guilty and is sentenced to hang.
1877	On March 1, Jack McCall is hanged.
1879	On September 3, Hickok is reburied on Mount Moriah, his final resting place.

Glossary

abolitionists (a-buh-LIH-shun-ists) Men and women who worked to end slavery.

acquitted (uh-KWIT-ed) To have been set free in a court of law from criminal charges.

adulation (a-juh-LAY-shun) Great flattery or praise.

ambush (AM-bush) A trap in which people hide and lie in wait to attack by surprise.

ammunition (am-yoo-NIH-shun) Things fired from weapons, such as bullets.

bail (BAYL) Money paid to a court to secure the temporary release of a prisoner awaiting trial.

bowie knife (BOO-ee NYF) A single-edged, curved hunting knife.

campaign (kam-PAYN) A plan to get a certain result.

cardsharps (KARD-sharps) People who cheat others out of money in card games.

cavalry (KA-vul-ree) The part of an army that rides and fights on horseback.

census (SEN-sus) An official count of people in various places.

civilian (sih-VIL-yin) Having to do with a person who is not in the military.

Confederate (kun-FEH-duh-ret) Relating to the group of people who made up the Confederate States of America.

constables (KON-stuh-bulz) Minor court officers, sometimes the equals of policemen.

counterfeiting (KOWN-tur-fit-ing) Copying something, such as bank notes, in order to deceive.

cow town (KOW TOWN) A town that serves as a market center or shipping point for cattle.

deputy (DEP-yoo-tee) A second in command or an assistant who has the power to act and to make people follow the law.

desperado (des-peh-RAH-doh) A reckless individual or an outlaw.

dime novels (DYM NAH-vulz) Cheap, fictional books of adventures in the Wild West.

enthralled (in-THROLD) Charmed or interested in something.

exaggerated (eg-ZA-juh-rayt-ed) Stretched beyond the truth.

frontiersman (frun-TEERZ-mun) A man who lives and works in an area that has not yet been settled.

guerrilla (guh-RIH-luh) Describing a small, defensive force of irregular soldiers.

gunfighter (GUN-fy-ter) A person who fights with pistols.

holstered (HOHL-sterd) Carried in a leather or fabric case specially made for holding a weapon and worn on the body.

interpreted (in-TER-prut-ed) Understood or explained the sense of.

lariat (LAR-ee-ut) A long rope with a loop at the end, used to catch livestock.

magistrates (MA-jih-strayts) Officials who make sure that laws are obeyed.

manslaughter (MAN-slaw-ter) Killing a person by accident.

marshal (MAR-shul) An officer of various kinds.

massacre (MA-sih-ker) The act of killing a large number of people or animals.

missionaries (MIH-shuh-ner-eez) People sent to do religious work in a foreign country.

negotiate (nih-GOH-shee-ayt) To talk over and arrange terms for an agreement.

obituaries (oh-BIH-chuh-wer-eez) Death notices often found in the newspaper.

outlaws (OWT-lawz) People who have broken the law and are on the run from the law.

paragon (PAR-uh-gon) A model of perfection.

peace officers (PEES AH-fih-serz) A general term for men who were employed as marshals, sheriffs or policemen.

pneumonia (noo-MOHN-ya) A disease in which the lungs become inflamed and fill with thick liquid.

quartermaster (KWOR-ter-mas-ter) An army officer who provides food, clothing, and other items for soldiers.

railhead (RAYL-hed) The station at the end of a railroad line.

raucous (RAH-kus) Disorderly; wild.

stampedes (stam-PEEDZ) Wild rushes of frightened animals.

subpoenas (suh-PEE-nuz) Orders commanding a person to appear in court.

tall tales (TOL TAYLZ) Made-up stories.

teamster (TEEM-ster) A man who drove wagons pulled by oxen, mules or horses.

telegraph (TEH-lih-graf) A machine used to send messages through air waves using coded signals.

unscathed (uhn-SKAYTHD) Not injured.

vagrancy (VAY-grun-see) A condition of having no proper home or work.

vengeance (VEN-jens) Punishment for an injury or an offense.

vigilance committee (VIH-jih-lens kuh-MIH-tee) A group of citizens that works to keep the peace until one is elected or appointed by the state governor.

wagon master (WA-gun MAS-ter) A man in charge of a number of wagons and their drivers, or teamsters.

warrants (WOR-ents) Papers that give someone the authority to do something.

Additional Resources

To learn more about Wild Bill Hickok and the history of the American West, check out these books and Web sites:

Books

Green, Carl and William Reynolds Sanford. *Wild Bill Hickok*. New York: Enslow Publishers, 1992.

Krohn, Katherine. *Women of the Wild West*. New York: Lerner Publications Company, 2000.

Martin, Greg, et al. *Buffalo Bill's Wild West: An American Legend*. New York: Random House, 1998.

Web Sites

Due to the changing nature of Internet links, PowerPlus Books has developed an online list of Web sites related to the subject of this book. This site is updated regularly. Please use this link to access the list:
www.powerkidslinks.com/lalt/wbhickok/

Bibliography

Rosa, Joseph G. and Robin May. *Buffalo Bill and His Wild West: A Pictorial Biography*. Lawrence, KS: University of Kansas Press, 1989.

Rosa, Joseph G. *The West of Wild Bill Hickok*. Norman, OK: University of Oklahoma Press, 1982.

Rosa, Joseph G. *They Called Him Wild Bill: The Life and Adventures of James Butler Hickok*. Norman, OK: University of Oklahoma Press, 1974.

Rosa, Joseph G. *Wild Bill Hickok, Gunfighter: An Account of Hickok's Gunfights*. College Station, TX: Early West Creative Publishing, 2001.

Rosa, Joseph G. *Wild Bill Hickok: The Man and His Myth*. Lawrence, KS: University of Kansas Press, 1996.

Sagala, Sandra K. *Buffalo Bill, Actor: A Chronicle of Cody's Theatrical Career*. Bowie, MD: Heritage Books, 2002.

Index

About the Author

Joseph G. Rosa is an Englishman who, as a child, loved watching western movies. He graduated from this to writing books after carrying out intensive research on the story of the real West. His interest in Wild Bill Hickok has led to years of study in both England and the United States, where the Hickok family encouraged him in his efforts and allowed him access to their family archive.

He has also written a variety of other books on the West and on firearms used in the Old West. He regularly visits the United States to continue his research and to attend the annual Western History Association's conference. He has also served as president of Westerners International and is a member of several western societies in England and the United States. A fellow of the Royal Society of Arts, he is currently president of the English Westerners' Society.

Primary Sources

Cover (foreground). James Butler Hickok, photograph copied from tintype, circa 1858, believed to have been taken in Lawrence, Kansas, Kansas State Historical Society. **Cover (background) & page 92.** Deadwood City, photograph, 1877, Adams Museum and House. **Page 4.** James Butler Hickok, cabinet card, early 1870s, the Clark Sudio in Mendota, Illinois, once owned by Lydia Hickok, now in Craig Fouts' collection. **Page 7.** *Wild Bill*, engraving, cover of *Harper's New Monthly Magazine*, February 1867, Alfred R. Waud, Library of Congress, Rare Book and Special Collections Division. **Page 8.** *The Struggle For Life*, engraving by Alfred R. Waud, cover of *Wild Bill, the Indian Slayer*, published July 1867, De Witt's Ten Cent Romances, Library of Congress, Rare Book and Special Collections Division. **Page 11 (top).** William Alonzo Hickok, photograph, circa 1850, collection of Joseph G. Rosa. **Page 11 (bottom).** Polly Butler Hickok, photograph, circa 1860, Kansas State Historical Society. **Page 12.** James Butler Hickok's birthplace, photographed in the late 1920s, shortly before the structure was torn down and replaced by a monument to Hickok, photograph in the collection of Joseph G. Rosa. **Page 13.** *Ma-Ka-Tai-Me-She-Kia-Kiah,* lithograph, circa 1838, I.T. Bowen's Lithographic Establishment, Library of Congress, Prints and Photograph Division. **Page 19.** Map of Kansas and Nebraska, lithograph, 1855, by J. H. Colton, Library of Congress, Geography and Map Division. **Page 20.** *Jemison's Jayhawkers*, etching, 1864, by Adalbert John Volck, abolitionists under Charles Jennison, wrongly identified as "Jemison," attack civilians in Missouri, Library of Congress, Prints and Photograph Division. **Pages 22–23.** St. Louis, Missouri, lithograph, by A. Janicke & Co., published circa 1859, Library of Congress, Prints and Photographs Division. **Page 27.** Poster advertising land for sale, 1872, Library of Congress, Rare Book and Special Collections Division. **Page 28.** Jones & Cartwright letterhead, from a letter dated June 6, 1861, addressed to Horace Hickok, held in the collection of Joseph G. Rosa. **Page 30.** *James Butler Hickok*, tintype, 1863, Kansas State Historical Society. **Page 34.** David McCanles, photograph, circa 1859, Nebraska State Historical Society. **Page 36.** Pony Express rider, lithograph, circa 1860, Bufford's Print Publishing House, Library of

Congress, Prints and Photographs. **Page 38**. Affidavit, dated July 13 1861, Nebraska State Historical Society. **Page 41**. *Putting Upon Him*, engraving, W. Jewett, published in *Harper's New Monthly Magazine* in February 1867, Library of Congress, Rare Book and Special Collections Division. **Page 43**. *Are You Satisfied?* engraving, unknown artist, published in *Harper's New Monthly Magazine* in February 1867, Library of Congress, Rare Book and Special Collections Division. **Page 45**. *American Progress*, chromolithograph of John Gast's 1872 painting published by George A. Crofutt, circa 1873, Library of Congress, Prints and Photographs Division. **Page 46**. Fort Riley, Kansas, watercolor, May 5, 1862, by John Gaddis, Kansas State Historical Society. **Page 48**. George Armstrong Custer, glass-plate photograph, Mathew Brady Studio, National Archives and Records Administration. **Page 48**. Winfield Scott Hancock, photograph, taken between 1860 and 1865, Library of Congress Prints and Photographs Division. **Page 52**. Group at Fort Harker, photograph, taken September 27, 1867, by Alexander Gardner, Kansas State Historical Society. **Page 55**. James Butler Hickok, glass plate negative, 1867, by E. E. Henry, Leavenworth, Kansas, Amon Carter Museum. **Page 63**. Joseph Geiting McCoy, photograph, circa 1871, Kansas State Historical Society. **Pages 64–65**. Cattle herd, photochrom, circa 1912, Library of Congress, Prints and Photographs Division. **Page 66**. Abilene, Kansas, photograph, Kansas State Historical Society. **Page 67**. Cowboys in Willow Creek, Wyoming, photograph, taken between 1870 and 1890, Western History/Genealogy Department, Denver Public Library. **Page 74**. Saloon in Leadville, Colorado, photograph, created between 1880 and 1910, Western History/Genealogy Department, Denver Public Library. **Page 75**. "Shooting Afray," October 14, 1871, published in the Abilene, Kansas, *Chronicle*, Kansas State Historical Society. **Page 79**. Kansas City, Missouri, January 1869, drawn by A. Ruger, Library of Congress, Geography and Map Division. **Page 80**. Poster advertising the Grand Buffalo Hunt, from the collection of Joseph G. Rosa. **Page 82**. *James Butler "Wild Bill" Hickok, John "Texas Jack" Omohundro, William "Buffal Bill" Cody*, cabinet card, 1874, taken in Michigan, Buffalo Bill Historical Center. **Page 84**. Program for Scouts of the Plains, no date, held by Ethel Hickok. **Page 87**. Metropolitan Billiard Hall, photograph, Western History/Genealogy Department, Denver Public Library. **Page 89**. Martha Jane "Calamity Jane" Cannary, copy of cabinet card, made circa 1895, by Locke & Peterson Studio, held in Craig Fouts' collection. **Page 99**. Standard deck of poker or faro cards, made circa 1860-1870, by L. I. Cohen, New York.

Credits

Photo Credits

Cover, pp. 11 (bottom), 15, 24, 30, 46, 52, 56, 59, 63, 66, 75, Kansas State Historical Society; cover (background), pp. 92, 96, Adams Museum and House, Deadwood, SD; pp. 4, 89 courtesy of the Craig Fouts Collection; pp. 7, 8, 27, 41, 43, Library of Congress, Rare Book and Special Collections Division; pp. 11 (top), 12, 28, 80, 84, author's collection; pp. 13, 20, 22–23, 36, 45, 48 (bottom), 64–65, Library of Congress, Prints and Photographs Division; p. 16, Wilbur H. Siebert Collection, Archives of the Ohio Historical Society Library; pp. 19, 79, Library of Congress Geography and Map Division; pp. 33, 34, 38, Nebraska State Historical Society; p. 48 (top), Still Picture Branch, National Archives and Records Administration; p. 53 courtesy of National Archives and Records Administration-Central Plains Region (Kansas City); p. 55 courtesy Amon Carter Museum, Fort Worth, Texas; p. 58, Autry Museum of Western Heritage, Los Angeles; p. 62, Texas and Southwestern Cattle Raisers Foundation; pp. 67, 74, 87, Western History/Genealogy Department, Denver Public Library; p. 82, Buffalo Bill Historical Center, Cody, WY, p.69.2179.

Project Editor
Gillian Houghton

Series Design
Laura Murawski

Layout Design
Kim Sonsky

Photo Researcher
Jeffrey Wendt